WOMEN'S RESILIENCE IN FIJI
HOW LAWS AND POLICIES PROMOTE GENDER EQUALITY IN CLIMATE CHANGE AND DISASTER RISK MANAGEMENT

AUGUST 2022

ASIAN DEVELOPMENT BANK

© 2022 Asian Development Bank
6 ADB Avenue, Mandaluyong City, 1550 Metro Manila, Philippines
Tel +63 2 8632 4444; Fax +63 2 8636 2444
www.adb.org

Some rights reserved. Published in 2022.

ISBN 978-92-9269-685-6 (print); 978-92-9269-686-3 (electronic); 978-92-9269-687-0 (ebook)
Publication Stock No. TCS220337-2
DOI: http://dx.doi.org/10.22617/TCS220337-2

Note:

In this publication, "$" refers to United States dollars and "F$" refers to Fiji dollars.

Cover design by Cleone Baradas.

On the cover: Mother and child walking along an improved road under the ADB Third Road Upgrading Project in Suva, Fiji. Women in rural remote communities of Fiji are among the most vulnerable groups of people battling climate change and disasters in the Pacific. Addressing preexisting gender inequalities; improving women and girls' access to social and public services, markets, and education; and employment opportunities are key elements for strengthening women's socioeconomic resilience (photo by Eric Sales, ADB).

Contents

Tables, Figures, and Boxes

Foreword

The impact of climate change and disasters is contingent on various socioeconomic factors as well as country laws, policies, and decisions by policymakers. Gender roles and social inequalities in access to resources, care responsibilities, and lower levels of education systematically disadvantage women and girls, rendering them more vulnerable to the impact of climate change and disasters. Numerous reports have revealed the disproportionately higher mortality rates among women and girls during disasters, further highlighting that this area of work requires closer attention from governments and development partners.[*]

The Asian Development Bank (ADB) works with developing member stakeholders with a shared vision to strengthen approaches to address climate change and improve disaster resilience through investments in water supply, sanitation, irrigation, flood control, transport and energy, as well as to enhance knowledge sharing and cooperation with partners in the region. It is understood that a "business as usual" approach no longer works for tackling increasingly complex problems in Asia and the Pacific. A holistic and truly cross-sector and thematic approach is needed, with gender equality being a central consideration for the effectiveness and sustainability of climate change and disaster risk management (CCDRM) actions.

The Government of Fiji has long recognized the need for a coordinated and holistic approach that incorporates gender equality, particularly through the new Climate Change Act 2021 and other recent policy documents, such as the Ministry of Economy's Gender Equity and Social Inclusion Policy and Action Plan (2021–2024). Both recognize that gender inequality contributes to disproportionate climate change and disaster impacts on women and that gender and social factors create overlapping and interdependent vulnerabilities. In 2020, Fiji's Cabinet supported the introduction of gender-responsive budgeting through pilots run in two ministries. This is a critical step to enable the strategic allocation of resources for government priorities in future budgets.

ADB has been promoting "integrated approaches" and working to mainstream gender equality and women's empowerment in operations to support developing members in their efforts to become resilient to climate change and disaster. Improved gender equality and women's empowerment turn into positive benefits for many other development goals and targets. The ADB Strategy 2030 Operational Plan for Priority Two on *Accelerating Gender Equality* outlines a clear vision of gender equality as an effective means for achieving sustainable and inclusive growth, including in the area of climate and disaster resiliency.

This Fiji country report is part of a series of publications that applies the National Good Practice Framework presented in the regional report *Gender-Inclusive Legislative Framework and Laws to Strengthen Women's Resilience to Climate Change and Disasters*, to explore the extent of integration of gender considerations in CCDRM laws, policies, and plans in Fiji, the Lao People's Democratic Republic, and Mongolia. It was prepared under a regional knowledge and support technical assistance project on *Strengthening Women's Resilience to Climate Change and Disaster Risk in Asia and the Pacific*. The project specifically aims to increase the capacity of these three counties to develop and advance gender-responsive CCDRM national and sector policies and laws. It also contributes to the

---

[*] S. Brown et al. 2019. Gender and Age Inequality of Disaster Risk: *Research Paper*. UNICEF and UN Women.

wider thrust of the ADB Gender Equality Thematic Group to promote national legislation that supports women's resilience through gender-inclusive approaches to CCDRM.

This report is important as ADB commitments are turned into actions. In light of the increasing complexity of climate and disaster risk challenges in the Asia and Pacific region, it adds to the understanding of gaps, as well as good practices in CCDRM laws and policies, and provides recommendations for moving forward. This report should serve as valuable input to support government agencies and policymakers in Fiji to make country laws and policies gender-responsive and supportive to women's resilience to climate change and disasters.

Samantha Hung
Chief of Gender Equality Thematic Group
Sustainable Development and Climate Change Department
Asian Development Bank

Acknowledgments

This report is based on work undertaken under ADB Technical Assistance (TA) 9348-REG: *Strengthening Women's Resilience to Climate Change and Disaster Risk in Asia and the Pacific*. Overall, the regional project objective is to strengthen the capacity of policymakers in three countries: Fiji, the Lao People's Democratic Republic (Lao PDR), and Mongolia, and to make climate change and disaster risk management (DRM) policies, strategies, or financing gender-responsive. This Fiji country report on climate change and DRM law and policy frameworks is one element of the project, and similar reports have been prepared for the Lao PDR and Mongolia.

The report was prepared under the overall guidance of Malika Shagazatova (social development specialist) and Zonibel Woods (senior social development specialist) in the ADB Sustainable Development and Climate Change Department (SDCC). Support and contributions were provided by Alih Faisal Pimentel Abdul (TA coordinator), Nalini Singh (national gender consultant), and Ma. Celia A. Guzon (senior operations assistant). Consultants Robyn Layton (gender and law expert) and Mary Picard (climate change and disaster risk management/environmental law expert) drafted the report. The report was edited by Amy Reggers, gender and climate change consultant.

Special thanks to Samantha Hung, chief of gender equality thematic group, SDCC; Sonomi Tanaka, country director, Lao People's Democratic Republic and former chief of gender equity thematic group, SDCC; and Erik Aelbers, senior country specialist, Pacific Subregional Office (SPSO) of the Pacific Department (PARD), for their overall support and guidance in the implementation of the TA project.

The report benefited significantly from comments by Mairi Macrae and Emma Veve, PARD, and Erik Aelbers, Kristina Katich, and Hanna Uusimaa, SPSO.

Special thanks for the contributions of participants in two national workshops in Fiji.

Abbreviations

ARC	Australian Red Cross
CCDRM	climate change and disaster risk management
CEDAW Committee	Committee on the Elimination of Discrimination Against Women
CEDAW Convention	Convention on the Elimination of All Forms of Discrimination Against Women
CEDAW GR37	CEDAW General Recommendation No. 37 on Gender-related dimensions of disaster risk reduction in the context of climate change
DRM	disaster risk management
DRR	disaster risk reduction
EIA	environmental impact assessment
FAO	Food and Agriculture Organization of the United Nations
FWCC	Fiji Women's Crisis Centre
FWRM	Fiji Women's Rights Movement
GBV	gender-based violence
HRADC	Human Rights and Anti-Discrimination Commission
IFRC	International Federation of the Red Cross and Red Crescent
ILO	International Labour Organization
MWCPA	Ministry of Women, Children and Poverty Alleviation
NCCP	National Climate Change Policy 2018–2030
NDC	Nationally Determined Contribution (under UNFCCC/Paris Agreement)
NDMA	Natural Disaster Management Act 1998
NDMO	National Disaster Management Office
NDP	5-Year and 20-Year National Development Plan
NDRRP	The Republic of Fiji National Disaster Risk Reduction Policy 2018–2030
NGP	National Gender Policy
PDNA	post-disaster needs assessment
SPC	Pacific Community
UN	United Nations
UNFCCC	United Nations Framework Convention on Climate Change
UN Women	United Nations Entity for Gender Equality and the Empowerment of Women
VAW	violence against women
WPA	Women's Plan of Action 2010–2019

Executive Summary

Climate change impacts and weather-related disasters fundamentally threaten the capacity of Fiji to continue on the path of sustainable development. As a small island nation, Fiji is highly exposed to the impacts of climate change and weather-related disasters, intense tropical cyclones and storms, sea level rise, ocean warming and acidification, and the related hazards of floods, landslides, and drought. The Republic of Fiji spans over 330 islands with a total land area of 18,333 square kilometers (km^2).[a] One-third of the islands are permanently inhabited, and most of these are volcanic in origin. The largest islands of Viti Levu and Vanua Levu make up around 87% of the Fiji landmass and are home to about 90% of the population.

In Fiji, there are strong linkages between climate change and disaster risk. There is a sense of urgency for Fiji to respond to climate change and disaster risks due to the immediate human impacts and recovery costs of weather-related disasters, the vulnerability of coastal communities, floods, and damage to agricultural activity due to seawater intrusion. These hazards impact health, livelihoods, and industry (especially agriculture, forestry, fisheries, transport, and tourism), housing, infrastructure, poverty, and social cohesion. The future of Fiji depends on its citizens being resilient to sudden-onset disasters and adapting to permanently changed environmental conditions. Decisions about how to adapt to these changes impact social groups within the population differently. Gender inequalities influence the ability of women and men and different social groups to build resilience. Therefore, decisions must be informed by sex- and age-disaggregated data as much as possible.

Historical data on the differential impacts of disasters on men and women in Fiji have not been collected and published systematically. However, post-disaster needs assessments (PDNAs) find that the major direct impacts following a disaster are loss of housing and possessions, and damage to crops, agricultural production, and businesses. These impacts are highly disruptive to family life, livelihoods and employment and increase the risks of gender-based violence (GBV). It is in these areas that gender differences emerge due to the preexisting differences in gender roles and inequalities in access to economic resources to respond to and recover from disaster impacts. Women in Fiji experience more significant economic impacts from disaster losses due to lower incomes and extensive engagement in the informal sector, increasing their economic dependence on men following disasters. These findings may be extrapolated when exploring the gendered impacts of climate change and slow-onset climatic changes, where women's informal work—such as agro-based microenterprises—are highly exposed to weather changes and hazards, and where women do not have the protection of insurance or adequate access to finance.

While the overall progress of Fiji toward promoting women's rights and gender equality is noteworthy, persistent disparities remain and impact women's ability to build resilience to increasing climate change and disaster risks. There is gender inequality in labor force participation in Fiji, and a significant gender wage gap exists. On average, rural women earn 25% less than rural men. There is a significant urban–rural wage gap of 44.5%.[b] Sexual harassment in the workplace is also widespread, with a 2016 study commissioned by the Fiji Women's Rights Movement finding that 20% of women in full-time employment, 30% of women in part-time work, and 43% of women in casual

---

[a]   Government of Fiji. 2016. *Fiji Post-Disaster Needs Assessment - Tropical Cyclone Winston, February 20, 2016*. Suva.

[b]   International Labour Organization (ILO). 2016. *Centralizing Decent Work in the Response to Tropical Cyclone Winston*. Suva.

work had experienced sexual harassment in the workplace. Violence against women (VAW) is another significant gender inequality experienced by almost two-thirds of women (64%) aged 18–49 who have ever been in an intimate relationship.[c] Evidence also notes that disaster shocks exacerbate violence against women and girls.[d] These key gender inequalities inhibit women's socioeconomic development and are likely to intensify with increasing climate and disaster risks. Therefore, it is crucial to ensure that women and men move forward with increased equality of outcomes alongside the challenges of combating disaster and climate impacts.

This report conducts a gender analysis of the national legal and policy frameworks of Fiji to determine whether laws, policies, and strategies consider gender inequalities as they relate to climate and disaster risk and contribute to strengthening women's resilience. The laws of a country set the legal framework and provide the foundation to regulate a sector and guarantee fundamental rights and policies that should amplify legal provisions and implement legislative guarantees. A *National Good Practice Legislative Framework* was developed for the analysis in this report. The framework draws on (i) the *Committee on the Elimination of Discrimination Against Women (CEDAW) General Recommendation No. 37* on the gender-related dimensions of disaster risk reduction in the context of climate change (CEDAW GR37), and (ii) a report on best practice legal frameworks in Asia and the Pacific, which assists in selecting laws and policies related to the national approach to gender equality, climate and disaster risks, as well as socioeconomic development for gender analysis. The analysis of the selected laws and policies informed an assessment of the extent to which equality and discrimination concepts are explicit in laws and policies and how this affects women's resilience to climate and disaster risks. The report methodology included secondary data collection and analysis, support from stakeholder interviews, a country mission, and national workshops.

The analysis found a commitment to addressing gender equality and prohibiting discrimination in Fiji; these concepts from international law are imported into its Constitution. There is also a National Gender Policy (2014) and Women's Plan of Action. Further, increased commitment to gender equality in climate change action and disaster risk management has more recently resulted in gender-responsive law and policy development, including the Climate Change Act 2021, the National Climate Change Policy 2018–2030 (NCCP), and the National Disaster Risk Reduction Policy 2018–2030 (NDRRP). The Disaster Risk Management (DRM) Law does not mainstream gender as of 2021, although a new National Disaster Risk Reduction Management (NDRRM) Bill is under development and presents an opportunity for change toward more gender-responsive DRM. The only reference to gender and women in the NDRRM Bill (draft) is in the context of women's participation and the representation of vulnerable groups in decentralized disaster committees.

In addition to sector-specific laws and policies, the report analyzed several laws governing socioeconomic areas that can contribute to women's resilience building to climate change and disaster risk. The report focuses on three areas: (i) combating gender-based violence (GBV), (ii) improving women's access to assets, and (iii) improving women's access to decent work. The analysis of the laws and policies related to VAW demonstrates that more work needs to be done to ensure the concepts of substantive equality and nondiscrimination are made explicit. Further, an effort is required to link preexisting risks of GBV to climate and disaster risk. Analysis of access to assets—specifically land—found that despite its complex nature, land ownership and control of land use in Fiji needs to be critically examined from the perspective of gender equality. It also found that efforts to promote women's access to assets must be included in laws and policies related to climate change and disaster risk. Finally, the analysis of decent work revealed that international standards on equal pay for work of equal value had not been adopted. The minimum wage is not reaching women doing informal agricultural work. Despite the 2007 National Policy on Sexual Harassment, there remains significant underreporting of sexual harassment in the workplace.

---

[c] Fiji Women's Crisis Centre. 2013. *Somebody's Life, Everybody's Business! - National Research on Women's Health and Life Experiences in Fiji (2010/2011): A Summary Exploring the Prevalence, Incidence and Attitudes to Intimate Partner Violence in Fiji.* Suva.

[d] United Nations (UN) Women. 2014. *Climate Change, Disasters and Gender-Based Violence in the Pacific.* Suva.

In conclusion, the report found that while the Climate Change Act 2021 and the NCCP serve as a gender-responsive framework for women's rights and gender equality in climate change, DRM laws and policies do not fully incorporate and address gender equality risks and issues. Further, several key socioeconomic areas explored in the report fail to promote equality and nondiscrimination and are not linked to the increasing climate and disaster risks faced by the people of Fiji. Without a suite of policy initiatives and legislation to enforce commitments to gender equality, it is unclear how effective the newly enacted gender-responsive Climate Change Act 2021 and the NCCP will be in strengthening women's resilience to climate and disaster risks. The report includes a set of specific and general recommendations to address some of these gaps.

Specific Recommendations:

(i) Mainstream gender equality and the gender dimensions of disaster resilience in the draft DRM Bill.

(ii) Acknowledge the links between disasters and increased incidences of GBV in laws and policies and support increased implementation of appropriate responses and redress for survivors of GBV.

(iii) Develop practical guidance on gender mainstreaming in implementation and budget allocation for gender-responsive climate action under the Climate Change Act 2021, including adequate climate finance in place to meet the gender outcomes prescribed in the act.

(iv) Revise the Environment Management (EIA Process) Regulations 2007 under section 61 of the Environment Management Act 2005 to ensure women have equal roles in decision-making.

General Recommendations:

(i) Collection and analysis of disaggregated data need to be prioritized.

(ii) Develop gender mainstreaming guidelines on DRM and climate change to support the implementation of both the National Disaster Risk Reduction Policy and the National Climate Change Policy.

(iii) Develop guidelines on increasing women's participation in environmental decision-making.

1 Background

There is increasing global political consensus that the transition to climate change adaptation, climate and disaster resilience, and environmental sustainability includes increasing the number of women in climate and environment related decision-making and promoting gender equality as part of climate action and disaster risk management (DRM). Gender equality and social inclusion are increasingly seen as essential to a just transition. Key international treaties recommend or mandate the inclusion of gender equality indicators as part of the reporting obligations of State Parties and some treaty bodies are leading by example through gender action plans. Under the United Nations Framework Convention on Climate Change (UNFCCC), a gender action plan includes targets for increased representation and participation of women in UNFCCC processes, a gender balance goal at intergovernmental meetings, and guidance for State Parties in their efforts to integrate gender equality issues into their national commitments, reporting processes, and plans.[1] These efforts are translating into results; gender analysis of Nationally Determined Contributions (NDCs) in 2020 demonstrated that 50% of the updated NDCs have a reference to gender or women, compared to only 33% in 2016. Several Parties that did not refer to gender in their 2016 submission now include references to gender, some in substantive ways. All of the new NDCs (countries that had not submitted any NDC) include a reference to women or gender.[2]

Similarly, within global DRM efforts, the Sendai Framework for Disaster Risk Reduction, the Ha Noi Recommendations for Action on Gender and Disaster Risk Reduction, and the *Ulaanbaatar Declaration* of the 2018 Asian Ministerial Conference on Disaster Risk Reduction all recognize the importance of promoting the participation of women in decision-making in disaster risk reduction (DRR) and ensuring gender-sensitive policies for disaster risk management. The *Ulaanbaatar Declaration* specifically called on all governments and stakeholders to:

> "Promote full and equal participation of women in leading, designing, and implementing gender-sensitive disaster risk reduction policies, plans and programmes, through joint efforts by public and private sector, supported by appropriate legal frameworks and allocation of necessary resources."[3]

Early thematic linkages between climate change and disasters in Fiji have led to a high degree of policy coherence on these two issues and their interaction with sustainable development, aligning with the Framework for Resilient Development in the Pacific (FRDP).[4] The FRDP is a single integrated regional framework on climate change and DRM that succeeded two separate regional frameworks on DRM and climate change. It provides voluntary guidance to governments and other stakeholders toward the three goals of (1) climate resilience, (2) low-carbon sustainable development, and (3) more robust disaster preparedness, response, and recovery. Similar to the global frameworks previously mentioned, its priority actions include the objective to: "Strengthen capacities at all levels of government, administration and community through inclusive gender analysis, responsive decision-making systems and

1   United Nations Framework Convention on Climate Change. 2019. *Gender and Climate Change: Proposal by the President: Enhanced Lima Work Programme on Gender and its Gender Action Plan.* (FCCC/CP/2019/L.3). Madrid.

2   Women's Environment and Development Organization. 2020. *Gender Climate Tracker: Quick Analysis.*

3   Asian Ministerial Conference on Disaster Risk Reduction. 2018. *Ulaanbaatar Declaration.* Ulaanbaatar. p. 2.

4   Pacific Community (SPC), Secretariat of the Pacific Regional Environment Programme, Pacific Islands Forum Secretariat, United Nations Development Programme (UNDP), United Nations Office for Disaster Risk Reduction and University of the South Pacific. 2016. *Framework for Resilient Development in the Pacific: An Integrated Approach to Address Climate Change and Disaster Risk Management (FRDP) 2017–2030.* Suva.

human rights-based approaches to ensure effective delivery of development initiatives" (footnote 4). It also aims to remain consistent with other regional approaches, including the Pacific Leaders' Gender Equality Declaration 2012[5] and the 14th Triennial Conference of Pacific Women which—in its Outcomes and Recommendations Statement in April 2021—set out 13 actions for governments that promote gender equality and reduce the impacts of climate change.[6]

Furthermore, the Committee on the Elimination of Discrimination Against Women (CEDAW Committee) is the treaty body of the long-standing Convention on the Elimination of All Forms of Discrimination Against Women (CEDAW Convention). It sets out in General Recommendation No. 37 the obligations of Member States on the gender-related dimensions of disaster risk reduction in the context of climate change (CEDAW GR37). This outlines the requirement for national policies and plans to address gender inequalities, reduce disaster risk, and increase resilience to the adverse effects of climate change. The CEDAW Committee notes that the focus needs to go beyond climate change and disaster risk policies and plans to also include national socioeconomic development planning.

Despite growing recognition of the need to integrate gender equality and full and effective participation of women in climate change action and DRM, a 2020 United Nations Entity for Gender Equality and the Empowerment of Women (UN Women) report notes that inconsistencies remain in national legislation, policies, and plans.[7] Many countries still have gaps in integrating their gender equality and women's empowerment commitments in climate change and DRM legal frameworks, policies, and plans. These frameworks have a critical role in demonstrating national commitments, however the adequacy of such frameworks on gender equality is yet to be comprehensively reviewed. This report focuses on Fiji, which is part of a three-country series that includes the Lao People's Democratic Republic (Lao PDR) and Mongolia. It contributes to addressing this gap by providing the results of a comprehensive gender analysis of national laws and policies to understand if and how they include gender equality concepts and language to form a strong foundation for promoting women's resilience to climate change and disasters.

1.1   Introduction

Climate change impacts and weather-related disasters fundamentally threaten the capacity of Fiji to continue on the path of sustainable development. As a small island nation, Fiji is highly exposed to the impacts of climate change and weather-related disasters, intense tropical cyclones and storms, sea level rise, ocean warming and acidification, and the related hazards of floods, landslides, and drought. In Fiji, there are strong linkages between climate change and disaster risk. The Republic of Fiji spans over 330 islands with a total land area of 18,333 square kilometer (km²). One-third of the islands are permanently inhabited, and most of these are volcanic in origin. The largest islands of Viti Levu and Vanua Levu make up around 87% of the Fiji landmass and are home to about 90% of the Fiji population.

There is a sense of urgency for Fiji to respond to climate change and disaster risks due to the immediate human impacts and recovery costs of weather-related disasters, the vulnerability of coastal communities, flooding and damage to agricultural activity due to floods and seawater intrusion. These hazards impact health, livelihoods, and industry (especially agriculture, forestry, fisheries, transport, and tourism), housing, infrastructure, poverty, and social cohesion. The future of Fiji depends on its citizens being resilient to sudden-onset disasters and adapting to permanently changed environmental conditions. Decisions about how to adapt to these changes impact social

---

5   Pacific Islands Forum. 2012. *Pacific Leaders Gender Equality Declaration 2012.* Rarotonga, Cook Islands.

6   SPC. 2021. *Outcomes and Recommendations.* 14th Triennial Conference of Pacific Women and 7th Meeting of Pacific Ministers for Women. 27–29 April, 4 May.

7   UN Women. 2020. *Review of Gender-Responsiveness and Disability Inclusion in Disaster Risk Reduction in Asia and the Pacific.* Bangkok.

groups within the population differently. Gender inequalities influence the ability of women and men and different social groups to build resilience. Therefore, decisions must be informed by sex- and age-disaggregated data as much as possible.

Disasters and the social disruptions of climate change often have different impacts on women and men. Women have differential vulnerabilities to the impacts of climate change. Women are also key actors and agents of change in building more resilient communities. The Government of Fiji recognizes the gender-based vulnerabilities of disasters and climate change and notes that gender power relations determine the agency of women and men to respond to impacts.[8] Gender inequalities constrain all women's lives, and access to resources, income, education, and health present additional challenges for women to cope with disasters and respond to climate change. Yet women are active in identifying solutions to these obstacles, making them key participants in DRR and recovery, climate change mitigation, and adaptation.

Although there are many gaps in statistical data, much is understood about the gendered impacts of sudden-onset disasters in Fiji based on PDNAs, evaluations of response efforts, and case studies of particular disasters. Two issues dominated following Tropical Cyclone Winston in Fiji: increases in GBV in temporary shelter and affected communities,[9] and greater impoverishment of women in recovery and reconstruction.[10] The impact of gender roles and preexisting gender inequality in disaster contexts—and therefore appropriate responses for future preparedness—often require a nuanced analysis. Gender-based vulnerabilities to disaster impacts need to be identified and analyzed in national and local settings.

Official statistical data collection on gendered impacts of climate change has even more significant gaps than on gender and disasters.[11] The scientific projections of an increase in average global temperatures—even if Paris Agreement emissions reduction targets are met—mean that ecosystems and indeed human systems will face permanent changes.[12] Global warming is changing which crops can be grown and where, including forests; which livestock and fish will be viable given changes in sea levels, temperature, and acidity; whether water supplies can be sustained, as well as disease vectors such as malarial mosquitoes and crop pests moving into newly warmer regions.[13] The role of women in food production—through subsistence farming or growing crops for income— is likely to be significantly impacted. These projected changes create risks to food security for families and communities. Changes to coastal marine fisheries and reduced availability of fish stocks—a challenge due to the changing climate—disproportionately affect women whose livelihoods and food security rely on them: there is a projected 50% reduction in coastal fishery harvest by 2100 in the Pacific.[14] These impacts will be more slowly felt than extreme weather events and require more permanent adaptation responses in Fiji. In this respect, women's participation in decision-making concerning climate change adaptation and resilience-building, environmental and natural resources management, and development planning is critical.

Women and men should both be included and benefit equally in the pursuit of climate adaptation, mitigation, and DRM. Research notes that gender inequalities in key socioeconomic areas in normal times can impact the ability of women to benefit from climate action and build resilience.[15] In Fiji, structural gender inequality and discrimination against women exist in many socioeconomic spheres such as women's economic participation and

---

8   Government of Fiji. 2017. *Climate Vulnerability Assessment. Making Fiji Climate Resilient.* Suva.

9   Fiji Women's Rights Movement (FWRM). 2018. *Submission on National Disaster Management Act (1998) and Plan (1995).* Suva; International Federation of the Red Cross and Red Crescent (IFRC). 2016. *Unseen, Unheard Gender-Based Violence in Disasters - Asia-Pacific Case Studies.* Kuala Lumpur, Malaysia; IFRC. 2018. *The Responsibility to Prevent and Respond to Sexual and Gender-Based Violence in Disasters and Crises.* Kuala Lumpur.

10   CARE and Live and Learn. 2016. *Rapid Gender Analysis Tropical Cyclone Winston Fiji.* Suva.

11   UN Women. 2018. *Gender and Climate Change under the Gender Action Plan (GAP). Submission by the United Nations Entity for Gender Equality and the Empowerment of Women (UN Women).*

12   Intergovernmental Panel on Climate Change (IPCC). 2018. *Global Warming of 1.5 °C.* Geneva.

13   IPCC. 2014. *AR5 Synthesis Report: Climate Change 2014.* Geneva.

14   UN Women. 2014. *Climate Change, Gender and Food Security.* Suva.

15   UN Women. 2020. *Climate Change, Gender Equality and Human Rights in Asia: Regional Review and Promising Practices.* Bangkok.

political representation, as well as grave human rights violations such as gender-based violence (GBV). To address these issues and enable women to build resilience, gender equality and nondiscrimination principles need to be embedded in laws and policies and actively implemented in programs and activities related to climate and disaster risks and socioeconomic development.

This report analyzes key national laws and policies of Fiji to understand how they provide a legal foundation and explicit commitment to strengthening women's resilience. This is done by looking at the national commitments to promoting gender equality, analyzing climate and DRM laws and policies, and reviewing select socioeconomic areas that directly relate to building women's resilience, including GBV prevention, access to assets, and decent work.

1.2 Purpose and Scope

Gender differences in the impacts of climate change and disasters are related to both preexisting inequality and discrimination. Differentiated gender roles mean that hazards may impact women and men differently. In general, disasters exacerbate prior disadvantages, while climate change adaptation can provide new opportunities and potentially reinforce existing disadvantages. To minimize the adverse impacts of climate change and disasters and improve women's resilience to these risks, it is necessary to understand underlying gender inequality and discrimination against women.

This report conducts a gender analysis of key elements of the national legal and policy framework of Fiji to determine the extent to which laws, policies, and strategies consider gender equality and contribute to strengthening women's resilience to climate change and disaster risk. The report presents a framework for selecting and analyzing laws and policies. The framework draws on CEDAW GR37 and builds on a national framework approach developed in a regional ADB report on best practices in legislation.[16] A country profile is presented to set the context—including key climate hazards and a description of the situation for women in Fiji—with a focus on socioeconomic areas that impact resilience building. Then a gender analysis is conducted of a range of laws and policies relevant to disaster risk management, climate change, and areas of women's socioeconomic resilience. The report concludes with an analysis of the extent to which the laws and policies promote women's resilience and makes recommendations to enhance the inclusion of gender equality commitments in laws and policies to strengthen women's resilience to climate change and disasters.

The key aims of this report are to:

(i)   outline a *National Good Practice Legislative Framework for Strengthening Women's Resilience to Climate Change and Disasters* which governments can use to analyze laws, policies, and institutions related to climate change and DRM;
(ii) apply the framework and present the analysis for the Government of Fiji—in light of the national context and international standards—to determine how gender-responsive laws and policies are; and
(iii) make recommendations on how the government can enhance the commitment to gender equality through laws and policies that promote women's resilience through gender-responsive climate change adaptation and disaster risk management.

---

[16]   Asian Development Bank (ADB). 2021. *Gender-Inclusive Legislative Framework and Laws to Strengthen Women's Resilience to Climate Change and Disasters*. Manila.

1.3 A National Good Practice Legislative Framework for Strengthening Women's Resilience to Climate Change and Disasters

To achieve the first aim of this report, a *National Good Practice Legislative Framework for Strengthening Women's Resilience to Climate Change and Disasters* was developed. The framework draws on the Convention on the Elimination of All Forms of Discrimination Against Women (CEDAW Convention) and CEDAW GR37. The CEDAW Convention is a binding international treaty that was adopted in 1979 by the UN General Assembly and is often described as an international bill of rights for women. Consisting of a preamble and 30 articles, it defines what constitutes discrimination against women and sets up an agenda for national action to end such discrimination.[17] Fiji is a party to the CEDAW Convention but has not ratified the Optional Protocol to the convention (this will be elaborated further in section 2.1).

Given the global focus on climate change, disaster risk reduction, and the significant impact on human life and livelihood, the CEDAW Committee added CEDAW GR37 in 2018. CEDAW GR37 discusses how the different aspects of the CEDAW Convention apply to these risks and makes expert recommendations to State Parties on how to address each of them. It states:

> "the Committee has underlined that State parties and other stakeholders have obligations to take concrete steps to address discrimination against women in the fields of disaster risk reduction and climate change through the adoption of targeted laws, policies, mitigation and adaptation strategies, budgets and other measures."[18]

CEDAW GR37 underscores the general principles of the CEDAW Convention that are applicable: substantive equality and nondiscrimination, participation and empowerment, and accountability and access to justice. It notes special measures—such as disaggregated data collection by sex, age, disability, ethnicity, and geographical location and its use, policy coherence, capacity development, and alignment with extraterritorial obligations—that State Parties should prioritize in the pursuit of reducing disaster risk for women.[19] Overall, CEDAW GR37 outlines how an increase in women's resilience to climate change and disaster risks needs support from broader socioeconomic laws and policies as well as the realization of specific rights such as the right to live free from GBV, the right to work, social protection, and the right to health, among others (footnote 19).

Building on the general principles of the CEDAW Convention, the specific areas of concern under CEDAW GR37— and the report on global good practice and international standards—Figure 1 presents the *National Good Practice Legislative Framework for Strengthening Women's Resilience to Climate Change and Disasters*.[20] When the framework is in place, the institutional mandates, policies, and strategies have a solid legal base. They can in turn support gender-responsive resource allocation decisions and the use of gender analysis and gender mainstreaming in the implementation of the laws and policies.

---

[17] UN General Assembly. 1979. *Convention on the Elimination of Discrimination Against Women.* United Nations Treaty Series, vol. 1249. 18 December.

[18] CEDAW Committee. 2018. *General Recommendation No. 37 on Gender-Related Disaster Risk Reduction in the Context of Climate Change.* CEDAW/C/GC/37. para. 8.

[19] This report adopts CEDAW's recommended minimum standards of disaggregated data. This suggests data to be disaggregated by sex, age, disability, ethnicity, and geographical location as much as possible. The term "sex-disaggregated data" is simply used for brevity throughout this report.

[20] ADB. 2021. *Gender-Inclusive Legislative Framework and Laws to Strengthen Women's Resilience to Climate Change and Disaster Risk.* Manila.

Section 2 of the report is structured according to the framework. Section 2.1 analyzes the Constitution of the Republic of Fiji and national laws that promote gender equality and prohibit discrimination. Given the number of laws related to climate change and disaster risk, this thematic area has been divided and section 2.2 covers laws related to DRM, while laws related to climate change and environmental management are reviewed in section 2.3. Finally, national laws and policies that contribute to building women's socioeconomic resilience are analyzed and presented in section 2.4. While the full spectrum of laws and policies as set out in the framework cannot be addressed in this report, many of these thematic issues are touched upon throughout the analysis.

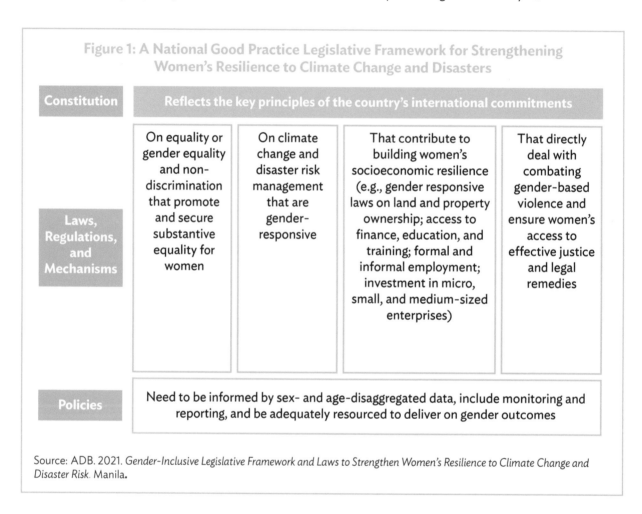

Figure 1: A National Good Practice Legislative Framework for Strengthening Women's Resilience to Climate Change and Disasters

Constitution	Reflects the key principles of the country's international commitments			
Laws, Regulations, and Mechanisms	On equality or gender equality and non-discrimination that promote and secure substantive equality for women	On climate change and disaster risk management that are gender-responsive	That contribute to building women's socioeconomic resilience (e.g., gender responsive laws on land and property ownership; access to finance, education, and training; formal and informal employment; investment in micro, small, and medium-sized enterprises)	That directly deal with combating gender-based violence and ensure women's access to effective justice and legal remedies
Policies	Need to be informed by sex- and age-disaggregated data, include monitoring and reporting, and be adequately resourced to deliver on gender outcomes			

Source: ADB. 2021. *Gender-Inclusive Legislative Framework and Laws to Strengthen Women's Resilience to Climate Change and Disaster Risk.* Manila.

1.4 Methodology

Desk-based research and gender analysis of selected laws and policies was the primary methodology in preparing the report, supplemented by country consultations, national workshops, and feedback on a draft report. Using the framework developed, there was a gender analysis of a selection of laws and policies from Fiji.

The gender analysis encompassed the following steps:

(i)   review the overall purpose of the law or policy;
(ii)   assess the relevance of the instrument to gender, its content, and its potential impact upon women, especially women's resilience;
(iii) look at the language used and determine whether it makes distinctions based on sex, gender roles, or gender stereotypes;

(iv) assess laws or policies on a continuum of gender integration from lowest to highest: from gender negative, gender neutral, gender sensitive, gender-responsive, to gender positive and/or transformative. Then classify them into three recurring categories: gender-responsive, gender sensitive, or not yet gender mainstreamed, with some additional specific references to gender positive and/or transformative examples; and

(v) make recommendations and/or highlight any good practices in the law or policy to enhance the commitment to gender equality through laws and policies that promote women's resilience in climate change and disaster risk management.

The purpose of classifying laws and policies on a continuum is to identify where gaps exist and where best practice examples can be highlighted. The continuum is adapted from the UN Women Training Centre[21] and WHO 2012 *Mainstreaming Gender in Health Adaptation to Climate Change Programmes*.[22] This analysis applies a three-point scale (color coded throughout) using authoritative international terminology:

(i) **Gender-responsive (green):** Pays attention to specific needs of women and men and intentionally uses gender considerations to affect the design, implementation, and results of legislation, policies, and programs.[23]

(ii) **Gender sensitive (yellow):** Considers gender norms, roles, and relations, taking into account sociocultural factors, but does not actively address gender inequalities.[24]

(iii) **Not yet gender mainstreamed (orange):** No attention to gender equality issues has been made, which may result in a gender neutral or a gender negative outcome.

It is important to note that the report refers to gender and gender-responsiveness as much as possible rather than to women only. This recognizes that laws, policies, programs, and actions affect both men and women and that sometimes gender roles can disadvantage women and girls and sometimes disadvantage men and boys, often in different ways. However, the report focuses specifically on women's resilience based on CEDAW GR37 and the gender-based vulnerabilities and risks to the realization of women's rights from climate and disaster risks. This aligns with the pursuit of gender equality and empowerment of women and girls under Sustainable Development Goal 5 and was articulated in the *Asia-Pacific Declaration on Advancing Equality and the Women's Empowerment: Beijing+25 Review*.[25] This report therefore primarily addresses how laws, policies, and gender mainstreaming can enhance women's resilience to these risks in Fiji.

1.5   Gender, Climate Change, and Disaster Profile of Fiji

The following profile highlights key disaster and climate change risks and dimensions in Fiji and presents a socioeconomic profile to provide the context of the gender equality situation.

1.5.1 Disaster Hazards, Their Impacts, and the Gender Dimensions

Fiji regularly experiences natural hazards of geological and hydro-meteorological origin (weather-related). In 37 years from 1970 to 2016, 124 disasters triggered by natural hazards occurred across most parts of the country, causing 480 deaths and affecting close to 3.3 million people.[26] This means that, on average, the people of Fiji experience three to four major disaster events over their lifetime.

---

21 UN Women Training Centre. 2017. *Gender Equality Glossary*. New York.

22 WHO. 2012. *Mainstreaming Gender in Health Adaptation to Climate Change Programmes*. Table 1, p. 10.

23 UNICEF. 2017. *Gender Equality Glossary of Terms and Concepts*.

24 WHO. 2012. *Mainstreaming Gender in Health Adaptation to Climate Change Programmes*.

25 United Nations Economic and Social Commission for Asia and the Pacific. 2019. *Asia-Pacific Declaration on Advancing Gender Equality and Women's Empowerment: Beijing +25 Review*. Bangkok.

26 Government of Fiji. 2020. *Third National Communication: Report to the United Nations Framework Convention on Climate Change (UNFCCC)*. Suva.

Figure 2 shows that the most people affected by major disasters during the same period have been impacted by tropical cyclones, floods, and severe storms (74%), while droughts have also significantly affected people over the same period, all from only six recorded drought events (26%) (footnote 26). The average asset losses due to tropical cyclones and floods combined are estimated at more than F$500 million per year, representing more than 5% of Fiji's GDP. At the same time, these losses also translate into an average of 25,700 people being pushed into poverty every year in Fiji.[27]

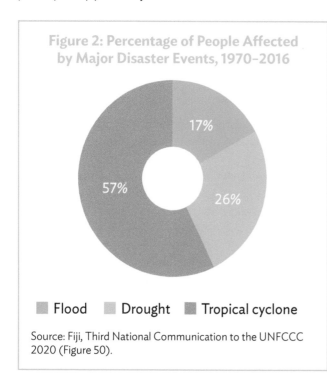

Figure 2: Percentage of People Affected by Major Disaster Events, 1970–2016

17%

57%

26%

■ Flood ■ Drought ■ Tropical cyclone

Source: Fiji, Third National Communication to the UNFCCC 2020 (Figure 50).

Given that disaster data is not regularly disaggregated by sex, understanding the gender dimensions of disasters requires relying on adequately disaggregated PDNAs and small-scale studies. Some available data are presented in section 1.5.3.

The frequency and intensity of cyclones in Fiji are significant barriers to economic growth and development due to individual impacts on health and welfare, jobs, and other economic activities. **Tropical cyclones** in Fiji occur on average twice per year: 66 tropical cyclones between 1970 and 2016 caused 355 deaths and affected nearly 1.89 million people.[28] Tropical cyclones result in unbudgeted recovery expenses and an estimated average annual asset loss of around 1.6% of the gross domestic product (GDP) (at first mention) of Fiji (F$152 million) (footnote 28). Asset losses from "100-year events" such as Tropical Cyclone Winston in 2016 can amount to over 10% of national GDP in a given year (Box 1) (footnote 34).

Floods—an annual event in Fiji—are caused by intense rainfall and regularly result in high economic losses. Such rains are also associated with dangerous landslides, especially with increased farming and settlements on hillsides.[29] On average, Fiji experienced more than one flood each year during 1980–2020. Flooding events are typically coastal floods (mainly occur during cyclones or tropical depressions due to higher tides and storm surges), fluvial floods (rivers bursting banks), and pluvial floods (swarming of drainage systems due to heavy rain). Floods cause widespread damage because most of the population and infrastructure are along the coast, on extensive river floodplains with long-duration flooding, or smaller catchments prone to flash flooding. (footnote 28). **Landslides** are also frequent throughout Fiji. As their occurrence and impacts are difficult to quantify, data relating to them is limited. Still, landslides triggered by rainfall events pose a significant threat to lives, livelihoods, and transportation networks (footnote 36).

Fiji has so far faced relatively short seasonal **droughts** lasting a few months or less. However, when a drought occurs, 20%–30% of Fiji's land area experiences drought conditions, posing a high level of immediate risk to agricultural production, livestock mortality, and access to safe drinking water (footnote 36). Six drought events during 1970–2016 affected 840,860 people (footnote 28). The indirect impacts of drought include forest fires, health impacts from poor water, and saline intrusions into rivers (footnote 37). As an island state, Fiji has a degree of

[27]   Government of Fiji. 2017. *Climate Vulnerability Assessment. Making Fiji Climate Resilient.* Suva.
[28]   Government of Fiji. 2020. *Third National Communication: Report to the UNFCCC.* Suva.
[29]   United Nations Office for Disaster Risk Reduction (UNDRR), Regional Office for Asia and the Pacific. 2019. *Disaster Risk Reduction in the Republic of Fiji. Status Report 2019.* Bangkok.

Box 1: Impacts of Tropical Cyclone Winston

In 2016, Tropical Cyclone Winston affected about 62% of the total population of Fiji. Its direct impacts were in the western and the northern divisions, with average wind speeds of 233 kilometers per hour (km/hour) (peak gusts over 300 km/hour) on Viti Levu, and storm surges that caused sea flooding up to 200 meters inland on Koro Island and the southern coast of Vanua Levu. It caused 44 fatalities and destroyed over 30,000 homes and many schools and health clinics. One in every five households lost a significant share of their personal belongings and had damaged or destroyed homes. Overall, the economic loss was valued at $1.3 billion, nearly half of which occurred in the aftermath of the disaster as the national economy struggled to recover. The agriculture sector suffered an estimated 65% of the total losses, which significantly impacted the country as 37% of households in Fiji derive some form of income from agriculture (crops, sugarcane, livestock, fisheries, and forests).

There were no significant gender differences in death or injury rates during Winston due to effective early warning systems. Differential impacts from Winston were heavily economic and disproportionately affected women. Interviews as part of the post-disaster needs assessment (PDNA) indicated that for women whose livelihoods were home-based —such as mat and basket weaving—the destruction of their homes and raw materials had a significant economic impact. Such agro-based microenterprises—which mainly comprise food processing, handicrafts and weaving—are at high risk from disasters as they are highly exposed to weather hazards and do not have the protection of insurance or access to finance. Many rural women also engage in small-scale fishing for family consumption and livelihoods. Winston destroyed many sand crab habitats mainly fished by women, resulting in disruptions and loss of income. This was significant, as alternative sources of income such as selling coconuts were also damaged. Women mud-crab fishers in Bua Province faced impoverishment as they had no access to credit services for loans, reducing their opportunities for income diversification after they lost equipment and access to their fishing areas. Further, as few people in Fiji can afford home insurance, rebuilding homes was a key challenge after Winston, which added to concerns for the safety of women and children throughout the reconstruction process.

Women in Fiji experience more significant economic impacts from disaster losses than men due to their lower incomes and extensive engagement in the informal sector, increasing their economic dependence on men following disasters. The Winston PDNA notes that "women are poorer, earn less income, are more dependent on subsistence economies, and, therefore, have fewer options to cope with the disaster impact than their male counterparts." The PDNA also identified increased GBV—especially domestic violence—as a high risk for all women in emergency shelters and their communities when their families had suffered the loss of income and damage to their homes, crops, and food gardens.

Sources: United Nations Office for Disaster Risk Reduction, Regional Office for Asia and the Pacific. 2019. Disaster Risk Reduction in the Republic of Fiji. Status Report 2019. Bangkok; Government of Fiji. 2020. *Third National Communication: Report to the United Nations Framework Convention on Climate Change.* Suva; Government of Fiji. 2016. *Post-Disaster Needs Assessment: Tropical Cyclone Winston, February 20, 2016.* Suva; Pacific Community (SPC). 2016. *Women in Fisheries.* Information Bulletin No. 27. Noumea, New Caledonia; UN Women. 2014. *Climate Change, Disasters and Gender-Based Violence in the Pacific.* Suva.

protection from **epidemics and pandemics**. The 2019 measles epidemic affected 14 people without loss of life.[30] The impacts of the coronavirus disease (COVID-19) pandemic are not yet fully known, although the economic impacts—especially on employment in tourism—are significant; the GDP of Fiji is forecasted to grow by 1.4% in 2021 after a decline of 5.8% in 2020.[31] Figures from 2020 show the decline in tourism has left 115,000 people (a third of the workforce, with around a third of them women) newly unemployed or on reduced hours.[32] Finally, **other natural hazards** that can also impact Fiji include the two active volcanoes in the region (low risk). At the same time, the volcanic soil of the larger islands is inherently unstable, adding to landslide risk, especially in areas

---

[30]   Centre for Research on the Epidemiology of Disasters. 2021. EM-DAT: The International Disaster Database (accessed 28 July 2021).
[31]   ADB. 2021. *Asian Development Outlook April 2021 Economic Forecasts.* Manila.
[32]   Government of Australia, Department of Foreign Affairs and Trade. 2020. *Fiji COVID-19 Development Response Plan.* Canberra.

where farming and settlement are spreading to fertile slopes.[33] Tsunamis and earthquakes are infrequent events that have not had a significant impact in recent decades. Still, when they occur, tsunamis pose a significant threat due to the number of low-lying islands (footnote 28).

1.5.2 Risks from Climate Change and the Gender Dimensions

Fiji faces a range of climate risks, significantly worsening some weather-related hazards and changes to the ocean such as sea level rise, warming, and acidification (Table 1) (footnote 28).

Table 1. Overview of Observed and Projected Climate and Other Disaster Risks in Fiji

Climate/Disaster Risk	Observed and Projected Changes
Sea level rise	Climate change models project that the sea level will continue to rise. Already some coastal lands and settlements are experiencing sea flooding or have been permanently inundated. The observed sea level trends for Fiji since 1993 show an increase of almost half a centimeter per year (4.7 mm). Longer term data is needed for accurate projections, but similar trends are being observed across the Pacific region.
Ocean warming and acidification	Based on climate modeling, both water temperature and ocean acidification are expected to increase.
Wave height	Climate change models project that wave height will decrease in the wet season, with a possible small increase in the dry season.
Tropical cyclones	Climate change models project that tropical cyclones will become less frequent but more intense. They have the most significant impact on the coasts, but due to the small islands, the whole country can be severely affected by widespread flooding, landslides, and storm-force winds, causing deaths to people and livestock and damage to infrastructure and agriculture.
Rise in annual mean temperatures	Average temperatures are projected to continue to rise, although relatively warmer and cool years and decades will still occur due to natural variability.
Extremely high daily temperatures above 35°C	Extremely high daily maximum temperatures are projected to become more frequent and become a normal occurrence by 2100.
Rainfall	The climate models indicate little change in annual rainfall but an increase in the wet season, with more extreme rain events. More year-to-year variability in rainfall is also projected under most models.
Floods: coastal, river, and drainage overflow due to heavy rain	Floods are common occurrences and are expected to increase, leading to large and growing economic losses. River floods (alluvial) and urban floods due to heavy rainfall overloading drainage systems (fluvial) are likely to increase due to the higher intensity of wet season rainfall. Coastal floods are likely to increase due to sea level rise.
Drought	Droughts are low frequency but high impact events in Fiji. Most climate models project a slight decrease in the proportion of time in drought, but there is a high level of uncertainty.
Geophysical disaster risks	There is some risk that earthquakes in Fiji's territory or other locations in Asia and the Pacific could give rise to tsunamis. Sea level rise will increase the portion of the population and assets exposed to tsunamis.

Source: Government of Fiji. 2020. *Third National Communication: Report to the UNFCCC*. Suva.

---

[33]   UNDRR, Regional Office for Asia and the Pacific. 2019. *Disaster Risk Reduction in the Republic of Fiji. Status Report 2019*. Bangkok.

Climate change is an inherently complex set of phenomena, affecting diverse sectors and activities and operating at timescales that range from short- to long-term (Table 1). Projections of future impacts remain somewhat general, at the limits of scientific knowledge, and the degree of uncertainty in some areas makes it challenging to make long-term policy decisions. It is reasonable to conclude that climate change is likely to increase the intensity of all weather-related hazards in Fiji.[34] Flood severity is already increasing, and the severe impacts on fisheries and agriculture are a significant concern due to potentially decreasing livelihoods tied to coastal resources (footnote 44).

The two main types of policy response to climate change are generally described as mitigation and adaptation. In Fiji, mitigation efforts focus on reducing greenhouse gas emissions through renewable energy in hydropower, wind energy, and biofuels (from industry by-produce and agricultural waste), looking toward greater use of thermal energy in the future.[35] Adaptation in Fiji takes many forms, from changes in fishing practices to large-scale national infrastructure projects on renewable energy or flood mitigation and water storage. Given the impacts of sea level rise and storms on coastal settlements, another form of adaptation in Fiji is for people to move away from these settlements, under government-sponsored relocation of communities, or through spontaneous migration from degraded or inundated land, both of which have already occurred in Fiji.[36] This issue is high on the government's policy agenda (Box 2).[37]

The Fiji 2017 Climate Vulnerability Assessment identified priority areas that include building inclusive and resilient towns and cities, improving infrastructure services, developing climate-smart agriculture and fisheries, conserving ecosystems, and building socioeconomic resilience.[38] These priorities can be applied to adaptation projects and national and local decision-making on the environment, natural resource management, specific development projects, and more general development priorities. Women in Fiji already play an active role in adaptation in many areas—particularly in some rural communities—such as establishing and acting as the stewards of rainwater harvesting for both household and agricultural use, and increasing community economic prosperity in the face of drought and water shortages.[39] There are also other forms of adaptation that may be needed. Coastal fishing is especially significant for women for family consumption and income-generating livelihood.[40] Women in rural coastal communities access small-scale coastal and reef fishing to provide the primary source of protein for the household.[41] This form of fishing may cease to be available if the projected reef destruction from ocean warming and acidification occurs. Adaptation strategies include turning to freshwater aquaculture and more ocean-based tuna fishing as coral reef fish stocks reduce due to climate change. However, the changes required to women's traditional fishing practices would require new training, resources, and equipment.[42]

Adaptation measures also need to be based on a good understanding of women's work. For example, it is generally assumed that fishing outside reefs tends to be men's domain and that women undertake only subsistence fishing.[43] Recent research reveals that this underestimates and undervalues the contributions of women fishers and their

[34] Government of Fiji. 2017. *Climate Vulnerability Assessment. Making Fiji Climate Resilient.* Suva.

[35] Government of Fiji. 2020. *Third National Communication to the UNFCCC 2020.* Suva.

[36] Scholars Strategy Network. 2021. How a Community in Fiji Relocated to Adapt to Climate Change; A.E. Piggott-McKellar et al. 2019. Moving people in a Changing Climate: Lessons from Two Cases Studies in Fiji. *Social Sciences.* (8) 133.

[37] Government of Fiji, Ministry of Economy. 2018. *Planned Relocation Guidelines: A Framework to Undertake Climate Change Related Relocation.* Suva.

[38] Government of Fiji. 2017. *Climate Vulnerability Assessment. Making Fiji Climate Resilient.* Suva. Annex 1 (This identifies 125 interventions across the priority areas).

[39] Oxfam. 2017. *Addressing Water Shortages: A Catalyst for More Resilient Development in Fiji.* Oxford, UK.

[40] A.S. Thomas et al. 2018. Quantifying and valuing the critical role women play in Fiji's inshore Fisheries Sector. *SPC Women in Fisheries Information Bulletin.* 28:15–16.

[41] SPC. 2011. *Vulnerability of Tropical Pacific Fisheries and Aquaculture to Climate Change: Summary for Pacific Island Countries and Territories.* Noumea, New Caledonia.

[42] See Pacific Community (SPC). 2011. *Vulnerability of Tropical Pacific Fisheries and Aquaculture to Climate Change: Summary for Pacific Island Countries and Territories.* Noumea, New Caledonia.

[43] Food and Agriculture Organization of the United Nations (FAO) and SPC. 2019. *Country Gender Assessment of Agriculture and the Rural Sector in Fiji.* Suva.

Box 2: Early Experiences of Planned Relocations in Fiji due to Climate Change Impacts: The Gender Dimensions

The experience of a few government-led relocations in Fiji highlights a range of gender issues, including insufficient engagement of women in the process and unforeseen consequences for their daily lives. These are well-documented in some recent case studies and include:

(i)   the relocation of the entire Vunidogoloa village in 2014 from the shores of Natewa Bay in eastern Vanua Levu Island to a new site 2 km inland adjoining the main road, a move triggered by increasing tidal inundation, coastal erosion, and saltwater intrusion;

(ii)   the partial relocation of Denimanu coastal village to higher ground on Yadua Island situated off the western tip of Vanua Levu, following housing damage and land loss from Cyclone Evan in 2012; and

(iii)   the relocation of Tukuraki village in the highlands of Viti Levu due to devastation by three significant disasters in 4 years (a major landslide followed by Cyclone Evan in 2012, then Cyclone Winston in 2016). The Tukuraki relocation was done as a partnership between the Government of Fiji, SPC, and the European Union.

The gender issues identified—especially in the earlier relocations—were a mix of the general problems of insufficient participation by women in community decision-making, context-specific challenges, and many more positive outcomes for all women. For example, in later interviews with women in both Vunidogoloa and Denimanu, some expressed the view that the men decided to relocate and that they had no choice or a voice in the process. The Vundidogoloa removal had positive benefits of increased housing quality, safety, and access to tap water in each house, which saved the women time queuing for communal water. On the other hand, the women became more reliant on their husbands to feed their families, as they could no longer fish every day due to the long distance from the new site to the sea. The Vunidogoloa houses also did not include indoor kitchens as promised, which meant that villagers had to build kitchens themselves. In Denimanu, the new housing site was not as suitable as planners thought, resulting in erosion and issues with septic systems and toilet blockages that resulted in health problems for some women. However, in Tukuraki, the new site was well chosen and prepared, the construction of homes met building approval standards, and it is closer to the school. It includes a community hall/evacuation center built to withstand a Category 5 cyclone, and rainwater harvesting with best practice water and sanitation. The small community was deeply involved, and none of the published commentaries has highlighted any negative consequences for women.

Sources: Scholars Strategy Network. 2021. *How a Community in Fiji Relocated to Adapt to Climate Change*; A.E. Piggott-McKellar, K.E. McNamara, P.D. Nunn, and S.T. Sekinini. 2019. Moving People in a Changing Climate: Lessons from Two Case Studies in Fiji. *Social Sciences*. (8) 133; SPC. 2017. *Tukuraki Village Relocation Project*; SPC. 2017. *Tukuraki Village Relocates to New Site, Post Land-Slide Disaster*.

catch in the full range of habitats, including an increase in selling part of their catch.[44] Many women wish to modernize their fishing techniques and increase their income earning capacity in this sector. Their inclusion in training, access to new technologies, and climate change financing will be an important aspect of building their economic resilience in the face of climate change. As traditional roles change and urbanization increases—partly due to disasters and climate change—women also need access to new economic opportunities such as jobs in tourism and industry, and renewable energy production. This will be critical for inclusive adaptation and resilience-building in the future.

---

[44]   A.S. Thomas et al. 2018. Quantifying and valuing the critical role women play in Fiji's inshore Fisheries Sector. *SPC Women in Fisheries Information Bulletin*. 28:15–16.

1.5.3 Socioeconomic Dimensions of Gender, Climate Change, and Disaster Risk Management

This section presents a selection of the socioeconomic factors that affect women's resilience and response to climate and disaster risks: (i) involvement in governance and decision-making, (ii) relative health outcomes, (iii) education levels, (iv) the main economic sectors and types of employment of women, (v) general workplace conditions which include workplace sexual harassment, (vi) access to land and assets, and (vii) exposure to GBV:

(i) **Women in governance and decision-making.** While progress on economic empowerment has been slow, women's participation in political processes has been more promising at the national level. As of 2021, 20% percent of parliamentary seats were occupied by women.[45] Men also held most of the jobs involving decision-making and leadership. According to the *Annual Paid Employment Statistics 2018*, women only made up 34% of the 9,860 jobs involving decision-making and leadership. This included legislators, senior officials, and managerial positions.[46] Women's representation at the senior management level is very low, with men dominating decision-making in high-paid positions.[47] One illustration of this taken from the education sector in 2017 revealed that although 62% of teachers were women and 38% men, the proportions were more than reversed at the senior level, where 74% of head teachers and 83% of school principals were men.[48]

(ii) **Health.** There have been significant improvements in women's health, life expectancy, and maternal mortality rates during 2000–2018.[49] Life expectancy has risen slightly for both sexes (69.2 years for women and 65.6 years for men), although it is still significantly below world averages. Poverty is an important factor in the status of women's health. Although maternal mortality ratios for women with low incomes fell from above 800 per 100,000 live births to below 500 per 100,000 during 2000–2018, there are still significantly more maternal deaths among poorer women (footnote 49). These figures do not show the intersecting factors of age, location, or disability, nor aspects such as differences in access to healthcare and medical treatment. A 2015 study of 1,125 households across Fiji found that women overall were more deprived of healthcare services than men;[50] 40% of women and 30% of men did not receive healthcare the last time they had an injury or illness that otherwise required it (footnote 49).

(iii) **Education.** Fiji has attained high levels of participation (almost 100% primary, 80% secondary) and gender parity in school education for some years. Girls now stay in school longer than boys, and more women than men graduate from tertiary education.[51] In 2017, the net enrolment rate in secondary schools for females was 90.9% compared with 78.8% for males, and at the tertiary level, there were 18,773 females and 15,807 males.[52] In theory, this gives women a greater advantage in obtaining more highly qualified positions in employment and management than men. Still, the reality is different, as the following employment analysis demonstrates.

(iv) **Economic sectors.** The leading economic sectors in Fiji are agriculture (including forestry and fishing), services, manufacturing, industry, and—more recently—tourism and related industries. The percentage of employment of men in agriculture is slightly higher than women. There was an overall drop in employment in agriculture during 2000–2019 (after the European Union ceased preferential prices for sugar from Fiji), and the sugar industry is now being surpassed by tourism.[53] In 2020, 48.3% women and 51.7% men,

45 World Bank. 2021. *The Proportion of Seats Held by Women in National Parliaments (%)*. (accessed 28 July 2021).
46 Government of Fiji, Bureau of Statistics. 2020. Annual Paid Employment Statistics 2018. FBoS Release No. 4, 2020.
47 Fiji Women's Crisis Centre. 2013. *Somebody's Life, Everybody's Business! - National Research on Women's Health and Life Experiences in Fiji (2010/2011): A Summary Exploring the Prevalence, Incidence and Attitudes to Intimate Partner Violence in Fiji*. Suva.
48 Government of Fiji. 2018. *Fiji Data Provisions CEDAW Committee 2018*. Suva.
49 World Bank Group. 2020. *Gender Data Portal* (accessed 26 July 2020).
50 International Women's Development Agency. 2017. *Exploring Multidimensional Poverty in Fiji*. Melbourne.
51 FAO and SPC. 2019. *Country Gender Assessment of Agriculture and the Rural Sector in Fiji*. Suva.
52 Footnote 48; Embassy of the Republic of Fiji in Japan/Russian Federation/Philippines. n.d. Sectors Overview; World Atlas. 2019. *What Are the Biggest Industries in Fiji?*
53 Embassy of the Republic of Fiji in Japan/Russian Federation/Philippines. n.d. *Sectors Overview*; World Atlas. 2019. *What Are the Biggest Industries in Fiji?*

participated in at least one agricultural activity (crops and/or livestock, fishing and/or forestry), while in 2019, industry employed only 8.4% of the women and 15.7% of the men who were in employment.[54] By contrast, the services industry engaged 57% of the women who were in employment and 47.2% of the men in employment.[55] Women employees in agriculture, forestry, and fisheries engage mainly in floriculture and small-scale agriculture for home consumption and food processing and selling food at markets.[56] Moreover, their agricultural production tends to be considered a part of their household responsibilities.[57] Of formally employed agricultural workers, women make up only 17.5%, and women make up only 14.5% of paid family workers on their farms (footnote 54).

The most common forms of informal work for women are subsistence farming and fishing. In Fiji, 78% of all informal sector work involves agriculture, forestry, or fishing, and women participate in one-third of this sector (footnote 57). Fisheries contribute about 2.8% to GDP, and 9.7% to total export earnings and encompasses marine, coastal, and river fisheries.[58] Women are significantly involved in subsistence fishing. Women tend to fish in shallow-water reefs, lagoons, or estuaries for small fish and seafood for subsistence or income generation. In rivers and estuaries, women fish for freshwater prawns, freshwater eels, goby, and crabs.[59]

In the services sector—where more women are employed than men—women are concentrated mainly in the wholesale and retail trades, education, health, arts, accommodation, and food services. Women make up more than 40% of the workforce in each of those subsectors.[60] Manufacturing—an important sector that includes textiles, garments, and footwear—employs a significant proportion of women as garment workers. Women made up 51% of the civil service in 2013, the vast majority as nurses, teachers, dental assistants, and administrative officers.[61]

Tourism is critical for Fiji. In 2017, it became the largest sector in the economy and it represented 34% of Fiji's GDP. The tourism sector employed approximately 118,500 Fijians. Women comprise a third of the tourism workforce.[62] Most tourism jobs are at the minimum wage level, including cleaners, restaurant staff, and receptionists (footnote 60). Only a quarter of managerial and professional level positions are held by women(footnote 60). Women-owned micro, small, and medium-sized enterprises also benefit from tourism by providing services and products ranging from handicrafts to local artisanal food products and cosmetics.[63]

A final yet essential element of economic activity is unpaid care work. Care work in Fiji is predominantly provided by women and girls and includes cooking, cleaning, fetching wood and water, caring for children and the elderly, and community work. Gender differences in hours spent on unpaid domestic and care work stand at 39 hours for women and 14 hours for men aged 30 to 34.[64]

(v)   **Employment and working conditions:** Overall labor force participation shows considerable disparities between women and men. As noted, women's participation is a little over half that of men, with around 37% of women in paid employment and approximately 76% of men.[65] Women's labor force participation varies depending on whether they are in low, medium, or high-income brackets (Figure 3). The highest workforce participation is among women from low-income levels.

54   Government of Fiji. 2020. *2020 Fiji Agriculture Census*. Suva.
55   World Bank Group. 2021. *Gender Data Portal* (accessed 28 July 2021).
56   CARE and Live and Learn. 2016. *Rapid Gender Analysis Tropical Cyclone Winston Fiji*. Suva.
57   UN Women. 2012. *Rural Pacific Island Women and Agriculture: Evidence, Data and Knowledge in Pacific Islands Countries*. Suva.
58   Embassy of the Republic of Fiji in Japan/Russia/Philippines. n.d. *Sectors Overview*.
59   A.S. Thomas et al. 2018. Quantifying and valuing the critical role women play in Fiji's inshore Fisheries Sector. *SPC Women in Fisheries Information Bulletin*. 28:15–1; and A. Vunisea. 2016. The participation of women in fishing activities in Fiji. *SPC Women in Fisheries Information Bulletin* 27: 19–28.
60   ADB. 2015. *Fiji Country Gender Assessment 2015*. Manila.
61   Government of Fiji, Media Centre. 2013. Gender Equality in Public Service. 19 November.
62   Government of Fiji, Ministry of Commerce, Trade, Tourism and Transport. n.d. *Fijian Tourism 2021*. Suva.
63   COVID-19 Response Gender Working Group. 2020. *Gendered Impacts of COVID-19 on Women in Fiji*.
64   Women in Fisheries Network - Fiji. 2019. *Rapid Care Analysis Report 2019*. Suva.
65   World Bank Group. 2021. *Gender Data Portal* (accessed 28 July 2021).

Not only is there gender inequality in labor force participation in Fiji, but women also earn about one-third less than men.[66] On average, rural women earn one-quarter less than rural men. There is a significant urban-rural wage gap of 44.5%, which increases the overall vulnerability of the rural population to poverty.[67]

In terms of general workplace conditions, sexual harassment is a significant form of gender discrimination that impacts women in Fiji. A 2016 study commissioned by the Fiji Women's Rights Movement found

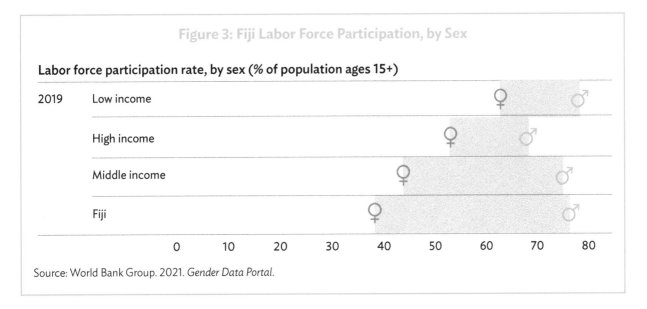

Figure 3: Fiji Labor Force Participation, by Sex

Labor force participation rate, by sex (% of population ages 15+)

Source: World Bank Group. 2021. *Gender Data Portal.*

that 20% of women had experienced sexual harassment in the workplace.[68] The highest level of sexual harassment was in the hospitality industry at 35%. Other sectors showing high incidence included 30% in the public service, 24% in health, and 23% in retail. The lowest rate was 8% in education. There were also higher levels of harassment reported by women in less secure employment. Of those in full-time employment, 20% of women reported sexual harassment, compared with 30% of women in part-time work and 43% in casual work. The study also found that women in junior or middle management were the most likely to have experienced harassment.

(vi) **Land and inheritance.** Generally, women in Fiji have the same legal rights as men to inherit and have access to land and non-land assets regardless of their marital status. While all women may be able to own land legally, some traditional inheritance norms and decision-making processes concerning land use often prevent this (footnote 60). Women are often excluded from the decision-making processes concerning communal land that makes up the majority of land holdings in Fiji. Traditional attitudes also mean that women are often dependent throughout their lives on their father or husband or male members of their family if they become widows.[69]

(vii) **Gender-based violence (GBV).** Almost two-thirds of Fijian women (64%) aged 18–49 who have ever been in an intimate relationship experienced physical and sexual violence by a husband or intimate partner in their lifetime. This is almost double the global average. The main forms of violence are physical, sexual, and emotional abuse by an intimate partner; sexual assault; and sexual harassment. Physical violence is the most widespread, experienced by 61% of all ever-partnered women, while 58% experienced emotional violence, and 34% experienced sexual violence. Women in Fiji aged 18–29 are at a much higher

66   ILO. 2016. *Centralizing Decent Work in the Response to Tropical Cyclone Winston.* Suva.
67   FAO and SPC. 2019. *Country Gender Assessment of Agriculture and the Rural Sector in Fiji.* Suva.
68   Fiji Women's Rights Movement. 2016. *Research Presentation: Sexual Harassment of Women in the Workplace in Fiji 2016 Follow up Study.* Suva.
69   UN General Assembly. 1979. *Convention on the Elimination of All Forms of Discrimination Against Women.* 18 December. United Nations Treaty Series, vol. 1249. para. 49 (b), (c), (e).

risk of experiencing intimate partner violence than older women.[70] The Government of Fiji report under CEDAW,[71] the NGO submission by the Fiji Women's Rights Movement (FWRM), and the CEDAW Committee's Concluding Observations emphasized the severe health and well-being costs to women of high levels of GBV in Fiji in normal times, aside from during or post-disaster situations.[72]

Overall, the socioeconomic profile of women in Fiji does not provide a good basis for women's resilience to disaster and climate risks, as women start significantly behind men in access to secure and well-paid employment, occupy few senior and decision-making roles, and suffer very significant levels of sexual harassment in the workplace and domestic violence at home. These forms of inequality and discrimination need to be addressed broadly as part of gender equality in national sustainable development, specifically through gender-responsive climate change and DRR.

[70] Fiji Women's Crisis Centre. 2013. *Somebody's Life, Everybody's Business! - National Research on Women's Health and Life Experiences in Fiji (2010/2011): A Summary Exploring the Prevalence, Incidence and Attitudes to Intimate Partner Violence in Fiji.* Suva.
[71] Government of Fiji. 2015. *Fiji's 5th State Report on the Implementation of CEDAW.* Suva.
[72] CEDAW Committee. 2018. *Concluding Observations on the Fifth Periodic Report of Fiji.* 14 March.

Laws, Policies, and Institutions Supporting Women's Resilience to Climate Change and Disasters

This section of the report presents the results of the application of the *National Good Practice Legislative Framework for Strengthening Women's Resilience to Climate Change and Disasters*. Each subsection includes an overview of the key laws, policies, and institutions, followed by the results and the gender analysis summary.

2.1 National Structure for Gender Equality and Nondiscrimination

A good national structure to promote gender equality and prevent discrimination against women should have laws that guarantee the fundamental rights of women. Policies should further amplify legal provisions and implement legislative guarantees. These fundamental rights should preferably be expressed in a constitution, as this supreme law sets the platform for all laws. It emphasizes their importance and provides a sound basis for interpreting all other legislation. The essential concepts of equality and discrimination need to be visible in laws (Box 3).

The framework presented in section 1.3 (Figure 1) presents five key areas for analysis. Two are addressed in this section: (i) the Constitution of the Republic of Fiji, and (ii) national laws that prohibit gender discrimination and promote substantive equality.

Box 3: The Essential Concepts of Equality and Discrimination

The fundamental rights of equality and discrimination—in relation to women—include the concepts of **formal equality** (equal treatment of women and men); **substantive equality** (equality of outcome or results for women and men); **promotion of equality** (taking positive steps to achieve substantive equality); prohibiting **sex discrimination** both **direct discrimination** (laws, provisions or requirements, which expressly disadvantage women in comparison to men), and **indirect discrimination** (neutral laws, provisions or requirements, which have the effect of disadvantaging women in comparison to men); **exceptions** to discrimination (making allowances for biological difference such as pregnancy); exemptions from discrimination (where discriminating characteristics are inherent requirements for a particular job); and **temporary special measures** (taking positive measures to redress historical disadvantages to women and bring about substantive equality with men). These essential concepts of equality and discrimination need to be set out in legislation with a sufficient degree of specificity and detail to be applied and enforced.

Source: UN General Assembly, *Convention on the Elimination of All Forms of Discrimination Against Women*, 18 December 1979, United Nations Treaty Series, vol. 1249.

2.1.1 Overview of Laws, Policies, and Institutions Related to Promoting Gender Equality and Nondiscrimination

Fiji has a single-chamber parliament.[73] The head of state is the President—whom the Parliament appoints—and the Prime Minister is the head of government appointed by the majority parliamentary party and who appoints the Cabinet of ministers from the Parliament.[74] The Constitution is based on a common law system of the doctrine of separation of powers: the Parliament (legislature), which makes the laws; the Executive (the public service comprising administration and policymakers); and the Judiciary (which interprets and applies the law).

The Constitution includes an extensive Bill of Rights. The Human Rights Anti-Discrimination Commission Act (HRADC Act) of 2009 provides a complaint mechanism for violations of both constitutional rights and the range of human rights in international conventions ratified by Fiji, including CEDAW.[75] Fiji does not have a general framework law that actively promotes gender equality. However, it implements many aspects of CEDAW through laws such as the Domestic Violence Act 2009, the Crimes Act 2009 and Criminal Procedure Act of 2009, the Family Law Act 2003, the Employment Relations Act 2007, and the Education Act 1966.

Policies that promote equality include the Women's Plan of Action 2010–2019 (presented in section 2.4.1 due to it being a focus of the 2019 report by the auditor general on eliminating GBV in Fiji), the Fiji National Gender Policy 2014 (NGP), and the *5-Year and 20-Year National Development Plan: Transforming Fiji* (collectively referred to as the NDP 2017). The NGP 2014—implemented by the Ministry of Women, Children and Poverty Alleviation (MWCPA)—has more than 100 activities in 19 key areas and shapes the government response to working with partners, stakeholders, and communities for gender equality, including ending violence against women and children.[76] The NDP 2017 consists of two prongs: (i) Inclusive Socioeconomic Development, and (ii) Transformational Strategic Thrusts. The Inclusive Socioeconomic Development prong aims to ensure all socioeconomic rights in the Constitution are realized. That inclusion will be the center of growth and development: "No one will be left behind regardless of geographical location, gender, ethnicity, physical and intellectual capability, and social and economic status."[77] The Transformational Strategic Thrusts prong addresses the new and emerging growth sectors to be nurtured, connectivity within Fiji and to the outside world, embracing new technologies and increased productivity.[78] Highlighted areas for improvement that are relevant to this report are: reducing the unemployment rate to below 4%; 100% access to clean and safe water and proper sanitation; and the consideration of gender as a crosscutting issue in the portion of the report on "Women in Development" (footnote 78). Thereafter, the 5-Year Development Plan—under the two prongs—sets out goals, policies, strategies, programs and projects, and the key performance indicators under each of the nominated topics. The NGP and NDP 2017 are analyzed from a gender perspective, and the results are presented in section 2.1.3.

Two characteristics of the Government of Fiji policy that are relevant to analyzing and drafting laws and policies are:

(i)   When referring to gender issues concerning women, the government prefers to use the expression "all women and girls" or "all women," as this includes intersectional aspects of women's rights, capacities, and vulnerabilities. The term is understood to include women and girls with different abilities, older women, and all cultures and ethnicities. Therefore, this report uses the preferred expression wherever possible in the context.

---

[73]   Parliament of the Republic of Fiji. 2021. *Fiji's System of Government*. Suva.

[74]   Government of Fiji. 2013. *Constitution of the Republic of Fiji 2013*. Suva.

[75]   Government of Fiji. 2019. *Human Rights and Anti-Discrimination Commission Act 2009 (Rev. 2016)*. Suva. Pub. L. No. 11 of 2009.

[76]   Government of Fiji, Office of the Auditor General. 2019. *Report of the Auditor General of the Republic of Fiji: Coordination of Actions on Elimination of Violence against Women. Performance Audit*. Suva.

[77]   Government of Fiji, Ministry of Economy. 2017. *5-Year & 20-Year National Development Plan: Transforming Fiji*. Suva. p. 2.

[78]   Government of Fiji, Ministry of Economy. 2017. *5-Year & 20-Year National Development Plan: Transforming Fiji*. Suva.

(ii)   Instead of referring to "temporary special measures," which is the CEDAW requirement to redress historical disadvantages to women and bring about substantive equality with men, the preferred expression by the Government of Fiji is "positive measures" or "positive advances" to redress disadvantages to women. Accommodation has been made to use those or similar expressions in this report wherever possible in the context. At the same time, it is noted that the CEDAW Committee Concluding Recommendations 2018 made specific recommendations about Fiji on introducing temporary special measures.[79]

The most important institution for promoting gender equality and nondiscrimination is the Human Rights and Anti-Discrimination Commission (HRADC). It is a high-level body set up under section 45 of the Constitution and comprises a chairperson (who must be a person who is or is qualified to be appointed as a judge) and four other members. The President makes the appointments of Fiji on the advice of the Constitutional Offices Commission. The HRADC 2018 Annual Report stated that the commission was committed to regaining its independent accreditation by ensuring that it complies with the "Paris Principles" (international minimum standards for effective and credible national human rights commissions)[80] and continues engagement with the Asia Pacific Forum of National Human Rights Institutions as well as the Global Alliance of National Human Rights Institutions.[81] This is a highly important goal for the commission to attain and give credibility and assurance to Fiji citizens.

2.1.2 The Constitution of the Republic of Fiji

The Constitution of the Republic of Fiji establishes the system of government and law-making of Fiji, and all other laws must comply with it.[82] Under section 51, international law and treaties are not automatically part of national law but must be approved by Parliament, which Fiji did for CEDAW in 1995. There is an extensive bill of rights in the Constitution in Chapter 2, sections 6–45. Two particularly relevant sections concerning this analysis are section 20 on the right to freedom of choice in work and decent employment, and section 26 on the right to equality and freedom from discrimination. Section 26.1 provides that "Every person is equal before the law and has the right to equal protection, treatment and benefit of the law," while Section 26.2 provides "Equality includes the full and equal enjoyment of all rights and freedoms recognized in this Chapter or any other written law." These two subsections give formal equality but not substantive equality (Box 3).

Section 26(3)(a) of the Constitution is a good practice example of a definition of unfair discrimination in many respects. It prohibits both direct and indirect discrimination and also sets out a broad range of prohibited grounds of "actual or supposed personal characteristics or circumstances," including race, culture, ethnic or social origin, color, place of origin, sex, gender, sexual orientation, gender identity and expression, birth, primary language, economic or social or health status, disability, age, religion, conscience, marital status, and pregnancy, as well as opinions and beliefs. However, the CEDAW Committee has noted that this definition does not explicitly define "discrimination against women."[83]

Section 26(7) of the Constitution importantly provides that treating another person differently on any of the named grounds is discrimination unless it can "be established that the difference in treatment is not unfair in the circumstances." It provides a defense that allows exceptions, although no particularity is given to the scope of "unfair" which is expressed very broadly. It is followed by Section 26(8) which provides for specific exceptions to "a law, or an administrative action taken under a law," that is not to be regarded as inconsistent with the rights in section 26. One such exception is Section 28(8)(g) "to the extent necessary and without infringing the rights or freedoms set out in any other section of this Chapter, gives effect to the communal ownership of *iTaukei, Rotuman*

79   CEDAW. 2018. *Concluding Observations on the Fifth Periodic Report of Fiji.* CEDAW/C/FJI/CO/5 (14 March). paras. 23, 24, 36, and 39.
80   United Nations Office of the High Commissioner for Human Rights. 2021. *UN Human Rights and NHRIs.*
81   Government of Fiji, Fiji Human Rights and Anti-Discrimination Commission. 2018. *Annual Report 2018: Neither Greater nor Lesser but EQUAL: Dignity, Equality and Freedom for All in Fiji.* Suva.
82   Footnote 74.
83   CEDAW. 2018. *Concluding Observations on the Fifth Periodic Report of Fiji.* CEDAW/C/FJI/CO/5 (14 March). para. 14.

and *Banaban* lands and access to marine resources, or the bestowing of *iTaukei, Rotuman,* and *Banaban* chiefly title or rank." Another exception is Section 26(8)(e), which exempts provisions regarding adoption, marriage, devolution of property on death, and pension.

Although Parliament has ratified and adopted the CEDAW Convention, it has not ratified the Optional Protocol to the CEDAW Convention, which would allow the review of individual complaints by the CEDAW Committee.[84] As of 2021, women in Fiji do not have access to an important avenue for individual action concerning complaints of inequality and discrimination to the CEDAW Committee. Also, in a similar vein, Fiji ratified the International Covenant on Economic, Social, and Cultural Rights and the International Covenant on Civil and Political Rights in August 2018, but has not ratified the Optional Protocols for those covenants. This means that some additional rights for women specified in the said covenants also cannot be enforced in Fiji. If women find themselves disadvantaged or without a sufficient voice in communal decision-making—especially with the impact of disasters and climate change, including relocation—Section 26(8)(g) of the Constitution can potentially support their right to gender equality within their community customary law. It leaves open the possibility that if customary law is discriminatory according to CEDAW, then the right to gender equality could be asserted by community members over customary law.

2.1.3 Gender Analysis Summary of Key Laws and Policies on Gender Equality and Nondiscrimination

A gender analysis was conducted of the key laws and policies to promote gender equality and prevent discrimination (Table 2). The color coded system is used to categorize the laws and policies and demonstrates the state of gender mainstreaming as of 2021.

Table 2. Summary of the Gender Equality and Nondiscrimination Framework

Law/Policy	Summary of Gender References
Human Rights and Anti-Discrimination Commission Act 2009	Human rights are articulated and reference is made to those human rights embodied in the United Nations covenants and conventions which the Republic of Fiji has ratified, yet there are no specific references to concepts of equality and discrimination.
Fiji National Gender Policy 2014	This policy discusses the need to promote and respect women's rights and makes particular reference to gender-based violence. The concepts of equality and discrimination are referenced as the principles of CEDAW as they relate to Fiji.
The 5-Year and 20-Year National Development Plan: Transforming Fiji 2017 (NDP 2017)	Gender equality is considered a crosscutting theme; specific reference to gender equality in the expansion of the rural economy is noted, including gender differences that exist for rural women. There is a goal relating to the collection of sex- and age-disaggregated data.

CEDAW = Convention on the Elimination of All Forms of Discrimination Against Women, NDP = National Development Plan.
Note: Color coding: gender-responsive (green), gender sensitive (yellow), not yet gender mainstreamed (orange).
Source: Asian Development Bank.

Results of the gender analysis found that the HRADC Act assumes that it would apply to men and all women equally and ignores that the act in its operation is likely to have a differential impact on women, who are more likely to be the subject of human rights infringements, notably discrimination and sexual harassment. Therefore, while the act implies equality between men and women, there are questions about how the act provides for substantive equality and the extent to which women are prepared to complain to HRADC. The 2018 Annual Report indicated that 192 complaints were received, and only one was expressed as discrimination against a woman, which was an eviction case based on pregnancy. There were 20 complaints regarding employment relations, but records did

---

[84]   As recommended as a priority by CEDAW in its 2018 Concluding Observations. CEDAW. 2018. *Concluding Observations on the Fifth Periodic Report of Fiji.* CEDAW/C/FJI/CO/5 (14 March). para. 10.

not indicate if the victims were female or male. The sex of persons should have been indicated in this report. In addition to complaints, none of the 126 inquiries, advisories, and requests for assistance were sex-disaggregated.[85] The absence of specific complaints being made based on discrimination against a woman—including sexual discrimination in the workplace—contrasts with the known prevalence of discrimination and sexual harassment of women in Fiji based on other sources.

The NGP, however, includes explicit direction on ending discrimination against women as well as specific objectives to "identify and strengthen institutions in Fiji which promote and protect the human rights of women, in particular relation to gender-based violence." This supports the National Women's Action Plan, which has the elimination of VAW as one of five key action areas (discussed in section 2.5). The NGP explicitly promotes equality and has the objective to "remove all forms of gender inequality and gender discrimination in Fiji."[86]

Under the NDP, the section on "Women in Development" (footnote 78). identifies many policies and strategies, annual targets, and key performance indicators on gender equality spread across a range of policies.[87] But generally speaking, there are limited references to women integrated into the NDP itself. Those limited references are under "National Security and the Rule of Law" and "Expanding the Rural Economy" which both refer to mainstreaming the NGP. References to women in "Expanding the Rural Economy" also point to equal access to agricultural production, with particular attention to gender differences such as access to land, repayment of credit, land purchase, land titling, public amenities, extension services, and technology, and also consider the disadvantaged position of the most vulnerable women in the rural areas (footnote 78). The goals refer to obtaining sex- and age-disaggregated data and increasing research on unpaid work in various sectors including agriculture (footnote 78). However, when addressing the economic sectors of manufacturing, commerce, fisheries, and tourism—where women are significantly employed—no mention is made of women. Although gender is referred to as being a critical crosscutting issue, there are few references to gender or women and girls in the NDP implementation goals, policies, strategies, programs, and projects, including the key indicators.

In the last decade, Fiji has taken significant strides to improve its institutional and policy framework aimed at accelerating the elimination of discrimination against all women and children and promoting gender equality. However, there is further work to be done to ensure that some of the institutions that have been set up, the policies related to gender, and the implementation of the various laws are truly having the effect intended by the government.

2.2 Gender and Disaster Risk Management

The impacts of disasters in Fiji affect women and men differently. Inequalities in women's access to land and assets—as well as structural and cultural barriers to participation in decision-making—are barriers to women's resilience building. Further, the increased risk of GBV as a result of disasters significantly hampers women's ability to bounce back from shocks. As such, laws and policies on DRM need to recognize inequalities and ensure the concepts of equality and nondiscrimination are explicit to support strengthening women's resilience.

---

[85]   Government of Fiji, Fiji Human Rights and Anti-Discrimination Commission. 2018. *Annual Report 2018: Neither Greater nor Lesser but EQUAL: Dignity, Equality and Freedom for All in Fiji.* Suva.

[86]   Government of Fiji, Ministry for Social Welfare, Women and Poverty Alleviation. 2014. *Fiji National Gender Policy.* Suva. p. 2.

[87]   Named policies include: increasing women's participation in formal sector employment (including reference to reviewing agricultural policies as well as income-generating activities under the Women's Plan of Action); increasing women's representation at all levels of government and civil society (which includes women's empowerment programs in rural areas, promoting girls training and participation in traditional male occupations, as well as collecting sex-disaggregated data to allow monitoring and evaluation of gender strategies); eliminating violence against women and children through improved policing; improving women's access to all social services; and finally reviewing of legislation and policies, notably the Family Law Act and regulations.

2.2.1 Overview of Key Laws, Policies, and Institutions Related to the Disaster Risk Management System

The system for DRM in Fiji is based on the Natural Disaster Management Act 1998 (NDMA), and an updated policy, the National Disaster Risk Reduction Policy 2019 (NDRRP). These are implemented by the National Disaster Management Office (NDMO). The Government of Fiji has undertaken wide consultations on revising the NDMA and relevant policies over recent years. As of December 2021, a draft National Disaster Risk Management Bill (draft DRM Bill) previously under consultation was being revised[88] and the NDMA remains in force.[89]

The NDMO is the national coordination center of government during times of disasters caused by natural hazards and in managing early recovery. It also has responsibility for awareness-raising and training on disaster preparedness, structural mitigation such as seawalls, and other matters, including recovery and reconstruction and post-disaster reviews from the national to community level (footnote 110). Situated in the Ministry of Disaster Management, the NDMO coordinates the national management of disaster activities. It conducts disaster management efforts at the national and subnational levels through disaster preparedness and disaster mitigation programs. The existence of the NDMO is mandated by law and was established by the 1998 National Disaster Management Act.

The Prime Minister officially launched the Republic of Fiji's National Disaster Risk Reduction Policy 2018–2030 (NDRRP) in December 2019.[90] This has effectively replaced the National Humanitarian Policy for Disaster Risk Management 2017 and the Fiji National Disaster Management Plan 1995. The NDRRP updates the policy approach to DRM in Fiji and sets the framework for the planned revisions of the 1998 NDMA through the National Disaster Risk Reduction Management (NDRRM) Bill that is under development.

2.2.2 Gender Analysis Summary of Disaster Risk Management Law and Policy

A gender analysis was conducted of DRM law and policy (Table 3). The color coded system is used to categorize the law and policy and demonstrates the state of gender mainstreaming as of 2021.

Table 3. Summary of Gender Inclusion in Disaster Risk Management

Law/Policy	Summary of Gender References
Natural Disaster Management Act 1998 (NDMA)	No reference to equality or nondiscrimination. The only reference to women or gender is the inclusion of the permanent secretary for women on the National Disaster Management Council, and on one of the three standing committees, the Preparedness Committee.
National Disaster Risk Reduction Policy 2018–2030 (NDRRP)	Gender is one of eight sets of policy guiding principles. "Human rights and gender-based approaches" are identified as a priority and the policy refers to obligations under CEDAW for: gender provisions in the NDP 2017, women as the most vulnerable groups, and the challenges of GBV in evacuations. No specific activities on equality and nondiscrimination appear in the seven technical sections of the policy.

CEDAW = Convention on the Elimination of All Forms of Discrimination Against Women, GBV = Gender-based violence, NDP = National Disaster Plan.
Note: Color coding: gender-responsive (green), gender sensitive (yellow), not yet gender mainstreamed (orange).
Source: Asian Development Bank.

[88]   SPC. 2019. *Fiji's Disaster Management Plan Under Review*. 28 August.
[89]   Government of Fiji. 2018. *Natural Disaster Management Act 1998 (Rev. 2018)*. Suva. Pub. L. No. 21 of 1998.
[90]   Government of Fiji. 2018. *National Disaster Risk Reduction Policy 2018–2030*. Suva.

The results from the gender analysis reveal that the NDMA does not set out any objectives or principles relating to women, gender equality, or nondiscrimination. It does not in other ways address the differential impacts of gender norms, roles or stereotypes, or preexisting gender inequalities, or provide for the empowerment of all women. For these reasons, it is classified as not yet gender mainstreamed. On a positive note, it does include the permanent secretary for women on the National Disaster Management Council, and on one of the three standing committees—the Preparedness Committee—but not on the Emergency Committee or the Mitigation and Prevention Committee. However, as all the council and committee positions are based on holding senior government roles—primarily permanent secretary level—these structures will simply reflect the gender composition of the senior civil service.

The NDRRM Bill under development provides an opportunity to establish a legal basis for gender-responsive disaster risk management. This could include elements such as (i) gender equality or nondiscrimination in its principles or objectives; (ii) specific provision for representation of women's organizations or a minimum percentage of women in the National Disaster Risk Management Council; (iii) gender equality in the staffing of the NDMO or employment of disaster service liaison officers; and (iv) guaranteed representation of women in Disaster Risk Management Councils at divisional, provincial, district, municipal, and communal levels.

The gender analysis of the NDRRP found significant consideration is given to gender as one of eight sets of policy guiding principles. The policy also refers to the Gender Action Plan adopted by the conference of the parties to the UNFCCC under Fiji's leadership, gender provisions in Fiji's 5-Year and 10-Year Development Plan, as well as Fiji's obligations under CEDAW. This—coupled with the references highlighted in Table 3—set a foundation for a gender-sensitive approach to DRM. The policy includes human rights and gender-based approaches as a policy guiding principle, however the technical sections that followed do not mainstream the principles into guidance on implementation, and this is an area where the policy could be strengthened. Mechanisms need to be put in place to ensure gender analysis and guidance for mainstreaming the principles into action plans and implementation, to ensure this will occur systematically and result in gender-responsive disaster risk management.

This report is timely in reinforcing discussions at the national level of the importance of a gender-inclusive DRM law to underpin the implementation of the policy and to go beyond regarding all women as a vulnerable group in disaster contexts. The Fiji Women's Rights Movement 2018 submission to the law revision consultation process emphasized the need to address key areas of gender equality in the law: GBV, the provision of emergency accommodation, the equal participation of women in decision-making processes, gender-sensitive and responsive resource mobilization, cross-sector coordination to address economic recovery, gender-responsive disaster response and the collection of sex-disaggregated data.[91] More work needs to be done to improve the gender responsiveness of DRM laws and policies in Fiji.

2.3 Gender, Climate Change, and Environmental Management

As a Pacific country made up of many small islands, Fiji is especially exposed to the impacts of climate change and weather-related disasters. The law and policy framework must deal with the increasing number and intensity of tropical cyclones and storms, sea level rise, ocean warming and acidification, and the related hazards of floods, landslides, and drought. The sense of urgency for Fiji is due to the immediate human impacts and recovery costs of weather-related disasters, the vulnerability of seaside communities, and damage to agricultural activity due to floods and seawater intrusion. All of these hazards impact health, livelihoods, and industry (agriculture, forestry, fisheries, transport, and tourism), housing and infrastructure, poverty, and social cohesion. They require the people

---

91   Fiji Women's Rights Movement (FWRM). 2018. *Submission on National Disaster Management Act (1998) and Plan (1995)*. Suva.

of Fiji to adapt to sudden-onset disasters as well as to changing environmental conditions. The abilities of women and men to adapt are different due to gender inequalities and discrimination against women as described in the country profile. This section provides an overview of the climate change and environment laws and policies, followed by a summary of the gender analysis conducted.

2.3.1 Overview of Laws, Policies, and Institutions Related to Climate Change and Environmental Management

The Constitution of the Republic of Fiji 2013 Bill of Rights provides the right to a clean and healthy environment. That includes the right to have the natural world protected for the benefit of present and future generations (section 40), which is relevant to general environmental management as well as to specific climate change laws. It is a reminder that Fiji environmental management laws will continue to have relevance in any discussion on climate change policy—including the gender aspects—especially because this legal framework is at the cutting edge of decision-making on the sustainability and community impacts of any significant development projects. For this reason, the Environment Management Act 2005 and its regulation on environmental impact assessments (EIAs) are included in this discussion and gender analyzed in section 2.3.2.

The key approach to climate change of the Government of Fiji is the Climate Change Act 2021. This comprehensive piece of climate legislation includes issues such as long-term net-zero commitments, carbon budgets, carbon market establishment, climate-induced human mobility, and nature-based solutions, and highlights the importance of resilience building.[92] Other policies are mentioned in the act—some of which are already in place—including the National Climate Change Policy 2018–2030 (discussed and gender analyzed in this section), the National Adaptation Plan 2018, the Low Emission Development Strategy 2018 (submitted to UNFCCC in February 2019), and the earlier Intended Nationally Determined Contribution 2015 (INDC) (the updated 2020 version of the NDC is gender analyzed in this section).

Other laws related to conservation and land, water, and natural resource management relevant to disaster and climate risk reduction and adaptation cannot be analyzed here due to time and space limitations. These include, for example, the Climate Action Trust Fund Act 2017 (Rev. 2019), the Climate Relocation of Communities Trust Fund Act 2019, the Environment and Climate Adaptation Levy Act 2015 (Rev. 2019), the Forest Act 1992 (Rev. 2006), the Fisheries Act 1941 (Rev. 2016) and the *iTaukei* Lands Act 1905 (formerly Native Lands Act) among others. There are several other environmental management and antipollution laws in place or proposed in Fiji not mentioned here.

Another policy required under the Climate Change Act 2021 is a set of guidelines on planned relocation due to climate change. This is a critical issue facing Fiji as a result of climate change and has already been a policy focus for 7 years since 2014. The government has developed the *Planned Relocation Guidelines: A Framework to Undertake Climate Change Related Relocation,* which is analyzed in the next section. The government released the first version of the guideline in 2016, and the most recent in 2018. It is described as a living document to be reviewed and updated as required. The guidelines emerged from government recognition of the need for relocation of communities based on observed and projected climate change impacts, including sea level rise, rainfall-related landslides, and cyclone damage. The government has decided to lead the process to ensure inclusive stakeholder engagement, proper planning and construction of infrastructure and housing, and consideration of socioeconomic issues before, during, and after relocation. The other policy analyzed from a gender perspective is the National Climate Change Policy 2018–2030. This is the key instrument providing vision, guidance, and institutional architecture to support climate-resilient development for Fiji.

---

[92]   Government of Fiji, Media Centre. 2021. *Fiji Legislates 2050 Net-Zero Commitment, Challenges Industrialised Nations to Follow Suit.*

The Ministry of Economy is responsible for regulating and coordinating climate change mitigation and adaptation, while environmental protection and environmental impact assessment of development proposals remain with the Ministry of Waterways and Environment. Local authorities also have key climate change prevention and risk reduction responsibilities.[93] It is useful to note here that the Ministry of Economy developed an internal Gender and Social Inclusion Policy in 2021 as part of the Green Climate Fund accreditation process and to formalize the ministry's commitment to equality and inclusion. This effort to link gender equality and climate action within the institution is needed and can further positively influence the implementation of policies and strategies.

2.3.2 Gender Analysis Summary of Key Climate and Environmental Laws and Policies

A gender analysis was conducted of select laws and policies relevant to climate change and environmental protection (Table 4). The color coded system categorizes the laws and policies and demonstrates the state of gender mainstreaming as of 2021.

Table 4. Summary of Gender Inclusion in Climate and Environmental Laws and Policies

Law/Policy	Summary of Gender References
Environment Management Act 2005 (Rev. 2018) and Environment Management (EIA Process) Regulations 2007 (Rev. 2016)	There is no mention of gender issues or any distinctions between men and women concerning environmental management issues. No statement of equality or nondiscrimination principles. The EIA Process Regulations require extensive consultation with "stakeholders" but there are no mentions of gender-inclusive processes.
Climate Change Act 2021	There are references such as "when taking action to address climate change Fiji will respect, promote and consider the Sustainable Development Goals, gender equality and responsiveness, women's human rights and the empowerment of women..." There is also mention of gender and inclusive processes in regard to displacement, where "to relocate at-risk communities only with the full free and prior informed consent of the communities, following inclusive and gender-responsive consultation and participatory processes," and to ensure nondiscrimination in this process. There is also mention of a gender balance when appointing representatives to climate-relevant committees.
National Climate Change Policy 2018–2030 (NCCP)	There is reference to inequality, gender responsiveness, and gender-inclusive processes. One of the purposes of the NCCP is to avoid exacerbating vulnerabilities or deepening gender inequality. There is mention of the need to increase women's participation and representation and plan to reduce gender inequalities.
Planned Relocation Guidelines: A Framework to Undertake Climate Change Related Relocation 2018	The guidelines mention gender equality and gender responsiveness as well as human rights. There is a commitment to "ensure an inclusive and gender-responsive consultative and participatory process."
Nationally Determined Contribution (NDC), updated in 2020	There is reference to gender responsiveness, improved gender balance in decision-making and implementation, and ensuring gender outcomes in climate action.

EIA = Environmental Impact Assessment.
Note: Color coding: gender-responsive (green), gender sensitive (yellow), not yet gender mainstreamed (orange).
Source: Asian Development Bank.

---

93   Government of Fiji. 2018. *Local Government Act 1972 (Rev. 2018)*. Suva. Pub. L. No. 4 of 1972.

The Environment Management Act and the EIA Process Regulations do not address gender issues or make any distinctions between men and women in environmental management issues. The EIA Process Regulations do require extensive consultation with "stakeholders" and in this respect, they represent good practice law. However, there is no requirement to undertake gender-inclusive consultations on new development proposals among the stakeholders. If the stakeholders are living in a village where community decisions are made according to customary law and practice, according to CEDAW, these should also be subject to scrutiny to ensure there is no discrimination against women.[94] The CEDAW Committee has held in some international cases that customary law discriminated against women in contravention of the CEDAW Convention.[95] As noted in section 2.1.2, the Constitution Section 26(8)(g) leaves open the possibility that if customary law is discriminatory according to CEDAW, then the right to gender equality could be asserted by community members over customary law. The Climate Change Act 2021 analyzed in this section makes a specific requirement that consultations for climate change relocation of communities must be inclusive and gender-responsive. The same principle should be applied to community consultations on development proposals under the EIA process, including "green development" and large-scale climate change adaptation and mitigation measures, to ensure that the concerns and needs of all women (as well as men) are taken into account in affected communities.

Human rights and gender equality in the Climate Change Act 2021 expressly import the rights and freedoms recognized in Chapter 2 of the Constitution and the link between gender equality and women's empowerment and sustainable development in the face of climate change Articles 5(a), 5(c), and 5(i):[96]

> "There are inextricable links between gender equity, social inclusion and the Sustainable Development Goals including the pledge that no one will be left behind, and when taking action to address climate change, Fiji will respect, promote and consider the Sustainable Development Goals, gender equality and responsiveness, women's human rights and the empowerment of women, rights of people living with disabilities and disability inclusive approaches, the elderly, children's inalienable right to a healthy environment, youth, and vulnerable and marginalised groups and communities, including in the areas of formal sector employment and livelihoods, participation in decision-making and access to services, health, education, water, sanitation, housing and transport."

The Fiji Climate Change Act 2021 is one of the most comprehensive national laws on this issue. It regulates climate change adaptation and mitigation and includes specific sections on climate change and resilient development, displacement and relocation, carbon sequestration, and oceans, as well as sustainable financing and private sector transition. In terms of gender equality and women's resilience to climate change it has the following key features:

(i)   The most important gender element is that there are principles set out in section 5 that must be applied by all the responsible persons and bodies whenever making policy and implementation decisions under the act:

    (a)   the bill of rights in Chapter 2 of the Constitution is included, with its right to formal equality and freedom from discrimination based on "sex, gender, sexual orientation, gender identity and expression," and other human rights;

    (b)   the "intergenerational equity" concept includes "socially and gender-inclusive, equitable" development; and

---

94   UN General Assembly. 1979. *Convention on the Elimination of All Forms of Discrimination Against Women*. 18 December. United Nations Treaty Series, vol. 1249. Specifically, Arts.1, 2(f), 3, 5(a), 14.2(a), (g), (h), 15, 16(1)(h).

95   S. Cusack and L. Pusey. 2013. *CEDAW and the Rights to Non-Discrimination and Equality*. *Melbourne Journal of International Law* (14); The Global Initiative for Economic, Social and Cultural Rights. 2012. *Using CEDAW to Secure Women's Land and Property Rights - A Practical Guide*. Duluth, MN, United States.

96   Government of Fiji. 2021. *Climate Change Act 2021*. Bill No. 31 of 2021. p. 19. Suva.

(c) it recognizes "inextricable links between gender equity, social inclusion" and the sustainable development goals—including the pledge that no one will be left behind—and makes a commitment that Fiji "will respect, promote and consider...gender equality and responsiveness, women's human rights and the empowerment of women" (and others identified) including in employment and livelihoods, participation in decision-making and access to services, health, education, water, sanitation, housing, and transport.

(ii) Review of the act: When the minister reviews the act every 5 years they are specifically required to consult with the minister responsible for women "on the extent to which gender principles are adhered to in all aspects of implementation"(section 10).

(iii) Some sections also require specific inclusion of women or their interests, or gender equality:

(a) the National Climate Change Policy must "embed gender, human rights, and social and cultural issues" (section 27);

(b) benefit-sharing plans for carbon sequestration must include women (section 60); and

(c) relocation of at-risk communities must protect women's rights and use "inclusive and gender-responsive consultation and participatory processes" (section 77).

Apart from Section 5(i) mentioned already, the term gender is used specifically in Article 10 mandating the minister to consult with the minister responsible for women on the extent to which gender principles are adhered to; on the promotion of gender balance in the National Adaptation Plan Steering Committee (Article 66[3]) and the National Ocean Policy Steering Committee (Article 82[4]); mandating gender-, age-, and disability-sensitive performance indicators to measure the effectiveness of the implementation of the act (Article 10[2]); and in Part 77(e) on the relocation of at-risk communities, where the minister is to "relocate at-risk communities only with the full free and prior informed consent of the communities, following inclusive and gender-responsive consultation and participatory processes." This is a very significant requirement because community consultations about relocation are a key part of the policy framework, and the specific inclusion of gender-responsive consultation and participation processes is essential for effective gender mainstreaming and empowerment of all women.

The structure of the act is such that gender inclusion is explicitly required; it is incorporated in many key sections by reference to the "principles of the act" from section 5 collectively. At key points throughout the act, the exercise of authority, decision-making, and policies are required to be consistent with the objectives and principles. Although gender equality, nondiscrimination, and women's empowerment are included as a principle of the act and mainstreamed into the policymaking as one of a group of principles that must be considered, there is no mechanism to require gender assessments or gender analysis, and most implementers will likely require further guidance in this regard.

The NCCP stands out as a good example of gender mainstreaming in climate policy. One of the purposes of the NCCP is to avoid exacerbating vulnerabilities or deepening gender inequality. The policy also includes gender responsiveness as one of its three key policy pillars, which is justified and expanded under seven points that can be summarized as:

(i) Women are agents of change and there is a need to improve and enhance the incorporation of all women's knowledge, skills, participation, and leadership into planning processes at the local and national levels.

(ii) Social adaptation is required, including addressing structural inequalities directly.

(iii) Benefits should be progressive and not reinforce the elements of traditionally and socially constructed roles for women and girls which contribute to gaps and inequalities.

(iv) There is a need to ensure that gender gaps are understood across government ministries and among stakeholders.

(v) It is necessary to plan for solutions that reduce inequality, through inclusive consultations and efforts that engage and incorporate all women's agency.

(vi) Use gender-sensitive indicators.

(vii) Recognize that natural resource management is not gender neutral.

The policy reiterates that it is "gender-responsive and human rights-based" and it includes a specific policy pillar on gender responsiveness as noted. However, in the later parts of the policy—including in the more concrete aspects of implementation—there is less guidance on how to ensure the gender policy pillar is mainstreamed. More work may be needed so that implementation is gender-responsive in practice and—for this reason—the policy is classified as gender-sensitive, but not yet gender-responsive.

Gender analysis showed similar results in the planned relocation guidelines. These guidelines draw on international best practice and lessons learned from Fiji's own experience of a small number of government-led relocations.[97] They are underpinned by a clear commitment to "ensure an inclusive and gender-responsive consultative and participatory process" set out in Part I of the guidelines. However, in the body of the document, this is usually shortened to simply "inclusive." This means that the detailed guidance on processes set out in Part II "Stages of Planned Relocation and Stakeholders Involved" does not specifically draw attention to gender inclusiveness. The detailed guidance on implementation does not highlight the gender component of "inclusiveness."

Finally, the updated 2020 NDC integrates gender equality issues in line with Fiji's newer climate policies. The NDC notes that planning processes for adaptation and mitigation will be guided by the principle of gender responsiveness and that gender issues, improved gender balance in decision-making and implementation, and gender outcomes will be ensured in climate action. Under the section on vulnerability and adaptation needs, there is another mention of targeted gender interventions as one way to reach the most vulnerable. Overall, there are explicit inclusions of equality and nondiscrimination language in the climate change law and policy landscape in Fiji, which forms an important benchmark for implementation and strengthening women's resilience to climate change risks.

2.4 Strengthening the Socioeconomic Resilience of Women

Strengthening women's resilience requires more than developing and applying gender-responsive laws and policies that are specifically directed at climate change and disasters. These phenomena occur within social and economic structures in which there are already different gender roles, as well as gender discrimination and inequalities that influence how disasters and climate change affect women and men. This subsection focuses on a selection of national laws that build women's socioeconomic resilience as outlined in the *National Good Practice Legislative Framework for Strengthening Women's Resilience to Climate Change and Disasters* (Figure 1). The framework includes laws preventing violence against women and girls, laws on land, inheritance, access to finance, education and training, and decent employment (formal and informal), among others. Given the enormous scope, the following three major themes were selected for their greatest immediate relevance to women's resilience to climate and disaster risk:

(i)   combating violence against women and girls;
(ii)   improving women's rights to assets; and
(iii) improving women's access to decent work.

These are all identified in the June 2018 *Ulaanbaatar Declaration*, adopted by the International Conference on Sustainable Development Goals: Gender and Development, as well as in CEDAW GR37.[98] The following subsections are presented as a discussion—not as summary tables similar to the previous sections—because there is often only one law or policy covering each area or in some cases several laws some of which have already been discussed.

---

[97]   See for example: UN High Commissioner for Refugees and Brookings. 2015. *Guidance on Protecting People from Disasters and Environmental Change through Planned Relocation*. Geneva and Washington, DC; and the most recent developments at Internal Displacement Monitoring Centre. 2019. *Global Report on Internal Displacement*. Geneva.

[98]   Government of Mongolia. 2019. *Mongolia Gender Situational Analysis: Advances, Challenges and Lessons Learnt Since 2005*. Ulaanbaatar.

2.4.1 Combating Violence Against Women and Girls

Violence against women (VAW) is a form of gender discrimination that reduces women's health and well-being, impacts their livelihoods through lost time in work or education, and increases their vulnerability to shocks. Overall, it inhibits women's social and economic capacity to reduce their risk, respond to and recover from disasters, adapt to climate change, and participate in emerging opportunities such as the green economy. As of 2021, there is little reference to GBV or VAW in the context of disaster or climate change laws or policies in Fiji, except for the NDRRP, which includes a section on the challenges of GBV in evacuations (discussed in section 2.2). The most relevant national law on the topic of violence is the Domestic Violence Act 2009 (Rev. 2016), and key policies include the Women's Plan of Action 2010–2019 (WPA) and the Fiji National Service Delivery Protocol for Responding to Cases of Gender-Based Violence 2018.

The preamble describes the purpose of the Domestic Violence Act 2009 as being,

> "to provide greater protection from domestic violence, to clarify the duties of the police in that regard, to introduce domestic violence restraining orders and other measures to promote safety and well-being of victims of domestic violence and to promote rehabilitation of perpetrators of domestic violence and for related matters."[99]

The act uses broad definitions of domestic violence, although there is no specific reference to "psychological" and "economic" harm or "deprivation of liberty", which are considered good legal practice elements.[100] The act expresses that the safety and well-being of the victim are paramount, which is a good legal practice. The act provides expanded authority to police to investigate and prosecute cases of domestic violence. Fiji has had a long-standing No-Drop Policy since 1995, whereby matters reported to the police are pursued, even if a victim withdraws an accusation.[101] The Fiji Women's Crisis Centre (FWCC) reinforced this good practice in 2014 with police training.[102] It was also affirmed in the auditor general's 2019 recommendations, which urged that the police finalize the revised version and ensure that police are trained.[103] FWCC has recently reported significant complaints about the No Drop Policy implementation, reinforcing the need for ongoing police training[104] and improved access to justice for survivors.[105] Overall, the act assumes that it would apply to both men and all women equally, yet the act and its operation have a differential impact on women, who are more likely to be the subject of domestic violence.

The purpose of the WPA was to fulfill Fiji's obligations to international and regional commitments.[106] The WPA has five priority areas for the development and advancement of women in Fiji: (i) formal sector employment and livelihood, (ii) equal participation in decision-making, (iii) elimination of violence against women and girls, (iv) access to services, and (v) women and the law (footnote 127). The Department of Women (now the Department of Women, Children and Poverty) has been responsible for the implementation of the WPA. The auditor general of the Republic of Fiji undertook a comprehensive audit on the implementation of the WPA, in particular on the topic of the Elimination of Violence against Women.[107] An overall recommendation was that the Department of Women, Children and Poverty should ensure that the plans for the development of the next WPA are properly

---

99 Government of Fiji. 2016. *Domestic Violence Act 2009 (Rev. 2016)*. Suva. Pub. L. No. 33 of 2009.

100 United Nations, Department of Economic and Social Affairs. 2010. *Handbook for Legislation on Violence against Women*. New York.

101 United Nations Population Fund. 2015. *Responding to Intimate Partner Violence and Sexual Violence against Women and Girls (Fiji)*. Manual. Suva.

102 Fiji Women's Crisis Centre. 2014. No-Drop Policy Reinforced. *Newsletter*. February–June. Suva.

103 Government of Fiji, Office of the Auditor General. 2019. *Report of the Auditor General of the Republic of Fiji: Coordination of Actions on Elimination of Violence against Women*. Performance Audit. Suva.

104 *Fijivillage*. 2020. FWCC Receives 240 Complaints about No Drop Policy Implementation but Police Say They Register and Investigate All Complaints. 6 February.

105 FWRM. 2017. *Balancing the Scales: Improving Fijian Women's Access to Justice*. Suva.

106 Government of Fiji, Ministry for Social Welfare, Women and Poverty Alleviation. 2010. *Women's Plan of Action 2010–2019*. Suva.

107 Government of Fiji, Office of the Auditor General. 2019. *Report of the Auditor General of the Republic of Fiji: Coordination of Actions on Elimination of Violence against Women*. Performance Audit. Suva.

aligned to the *Beijing Declaration and Platform of Action* and that strategic objectives in the WPA document capture what the action plans purport to reflect (footnote 128). This justifies the timely inclusion of a dedicated section in a revised WPA on climate action and resilience building, in line with the *Asia-Pacific Declaration on Advancing Gender Equality and Women's Empowerment: Beijing+25 Review*.[108]

Finally, the National Service Delivery Protocol for Responding to Cases of Gender-Based Violence by the MWCPA sets out the standard operating procedures for a coordinated response among social services, police, health, and legal/justice providers for GBV survivors. It outlines guiding principles, reporting, referral pathways, and the roles and responsibilities of each service provider. As of 2021, there is no evidence of how the protocol has been applied to GBV in a disaster context. However, evidence from Fiji and the Pacific acknowledges the significant increase in the prevalence of GBV during and after disasters and—importantly—the protocol references how to adapt GBV services in times of crisis and provides guidance on GBV referral pathways developed for emergencies and disasters.[109] Concluding observations by the CEDAW Committee from the fifth periodic report of Fiji also explicitly highlight the need for provisions for responding to GBV in the context of disasters, including establishing women-only disaster shelters and procedures for women to report GBV and access redress and rehabilitation.[110]

In 2021, Fiji was also in consultation on the National Action Plan to Prevent Violence Against Women and Girls (2021–2026), which is a 5-year plan intended to promote a shared understanding and whole-of-population approach to preventing violence. Targeted at primary approaches, the consultation includes 13 key settings, including a series of face-to-face and virtual consultations. One of these key settings is the informal sector, which includes women and members of the lesbian, bisexual, gay, transgender, queer, and intersex community who are involved in agriculture, horticulture, and fisheries and are at great risk of the impacts of climate change and disasters both economically and environmentally. The timeline for the National Action Plan launch was under review in 2021 in the wake of COVID-19 restrictions.[111]

The analysis of the laws and policies related to VAW demonstrates that more work needs to be done to ensure the concepts of substantive equality and nondiscrimination are explicit. Further, efforts to link preexisting risks of violence to climate and disaster risks are also critical, and evidence of the consultation phase of the National Action Plan to Prevent Violence Against Women and Girls is a promising step in this direction. The prevalence and nature of domestic violence in Fiji, as described in the country profile, points to the need to address this issue urgently. As part of this effort, data and evidence need to be gathered on the prevalence of VAW in the context of disasters and climate change.

2.4.2 Improving Women's Rights to Assets

CEDAW GR37 notes women—specifically rural and indigenous women involved in food and agricultural work—are directly affected by disasters and climate change. GR37 acknowledges that women make up the majority of the world's smallholder and subsistence farmers, and a significant proportion is farm workers; and that as a result of discriminatory laws and social norms, women often have limited access to secure land tenure. Moreover, the farmland women are allotted is often of inferior quality and more prone to flooding, erosion, or other adverse climatic events (footnote 132). Often women do not possess the legal and socially recognized land ownership necessary to adapt to changing climatic conditions effectively.[112] This includes not only the tenure of land but also how women may inherit land or housing. These themes are important in the pursuit to strengthen women's resilience to climate change and disasters in Fiji.

[108] United Nations Economic and Social Commission for Asia and the Pacific. 2019. *Asia-Pacific Declaration on Advancing Gender Equality and Women's Empowerment: Beijing +25 Review*. Bangkok.
[109] UN Women. 2014. *Climate Change, Disasters and Gender Based Violence in the Pacific*. Suva.
[110] CEDAW. 2018. *Concluding Observations on the Fifth Periodic Report of Fiji*. CEDAW/C/FJI/CO/5 (14 March).
[111] Government of Fiji, Media Centre. 2020. *Fiji to Develop a National Action Plan to Prevent Violence against Women and Girls*. 14 January.
[112] B.C. Prasad and S. Kumar. 2001. *Property Rights in Fiji: Women's Welfare and Empowerment*. Delhi.

In Fiji, land is a complex asset often governed by cultural traditions. There are three main categories of land types: (i) *iTaukei* land, 83% of which is inalienable under the *iTaukei* Lands Trust Act and cannot be transferred, charged, or encumbered by its customary owners; (ii) freehold land, meaning land which has been alienated by the state or by its customary owners and is now privately owned, 10%; and, (iii) state land (also referred to as "crown land"), meaning land held by the Government of Fiji, 7%.[113] Land tenure is a critical issue for women and it has been said that "the question of land itself is a prism through which structural patterns of gender inequality can be revealed."[114] Ownership practices are generally based on systems where males inherit property, which is true even in minority groups influenced by Islamic law that provides that female children inherit at least half of what their brothers inherit.[115] There are a few areas of Fiji where social groups practice matrilineal land inheritance, and women have some decision-making rights concerning land, however this is uncommon.[116]

Land is a fundamental aspect of social, religious, and economic practices. The amount of land that a chief controls indicates his status in society.[117] Communal land tenure has historically revolved around a man's relationship with the chief, who controls all land in the area.[118] Traditionally, community dispute resolution mechanisms have been that families on the land will come to a compromise and future agreement, prioritizing communal interests.[119] This method involves addressing the issues in a public manner and serves a restorative justice purpose, different from the adversarial court system.[120] Women's voices are not often considered equal to men's in these circumstances. However, land disputes predominantly go through the court system, and often the cases are prolonged due to the absence of substantive land information.[121] *iTaukei* land records and policies are not readily attainable and this, combined with the lack of an alternative dispute resolution system, has provoked calls for reform.[122]

In Fiji, the State Acquisition of Lands Act empowers the government to take possession of land during any emergency or calamity that threatens the life or well-being of the community.[123] If the government decides to exercise this power, it may take possession of the land immediately. It must, however, adhere to the strict procedures which include informing the landholder, who has a right to object. This is determined by a tribunal and includes adequate compensation paid to the landholder if compulsory acquisition applies.[124] These processes all involve males in the communities, and women might be left out of the decision-making processes.

Inheritance rights and housing are other key areas that are vital for women as they are connected to levels of poverty and inextricably linked with economic autonomy. These rights are highly important to strengthening women's economic resilience to disasters and climate change. In Fiji, women and men have equal rights to inherit under the Inheritance (Family Provision) Act (section 3) and the Succession, Probate, and Administration Act (section 6). However as noted, land inheritance traditions that favor patriarchal lineages can influence land inheritance practices

---

113   Government of Fiji, Ministry of Lands and Mineral Resources. Department of Lands.
114   The Global Initiative for Economic, Social and Cultural Rights. 2012. *Using CEDAW to Secure Women's Land and Property Rights—A Practical Guide*. Duluth, MN, United States.
115   B.C. Prasad and S. Kumar. 2001. *Property Rights in Fiji: Women's Welfare and Empowerment*. Delhi.
116   C. Bolabola. 1986. Fiji: Customary Constraints and Legal Progress, in *Land Rights of Pacific Women*. Suva, Fiji: Institute of Pacific Studies of the University of the South Pacific.; Australian Red Cross (ARC) and IFRC. 2018. *Disaster Law Housing, Land and Property Mapping Project: Fiji (Draft)*. Geneva.
117   ARC and IFRC. 2018. *Disaster Law Housing, Land and Property Mapping Project: Fiji (Draft)*. Geneva.
118   C. Bolabola. 1986. Fiji: Customary Constraints and Legal Progress, in *Land Rights of Pacific Women*. Suva, Fiji: Institute of Pacific Studies of the University of the South Pacific.; Footnote 117.
119   R.F. Ralogaivau. 2006. *Problem Solving Courts: Blending Traditional Approaches To Dispute Resolution In Fiji With Rule Of Law - The Best Of Both Worlds*. Paper presented to the 3rd Asia Pacific Mediation Forum Conference held at the University of the South Pacific, Suva, on Mediating Cultures in the Pacific and Asia. Fiji. 26–30 June; K. Fonmanu et al. 2003. Dispute Resolution for Customary Lands: Some Lessons for Fiji. *Survey Review*. 37(289). pp. 177–89.
120   Footnote 117.
121   K. Fonmanu et al. 2003. Dispute Resolution for Customary Lands: Some Lessons for Fiji. *Survey Review*. 37(289). pp. 177–89.
122   Footnote 117.
123   Government of Fiji. *State Acquisition of Lands Act 1940*. Suva. Sec. 8.
124   Footnote 117.

to exclude women. Women in rural areas may also be unfairly prejudiced by traditional customs in marriage.[125] This makes some rural women dependent on men throughout their lives: firstly, their father; then their husband; then—once they become widows—they depend on the goodwill of the male line in their father's family (footnote 60). While it is important—and indeed, a fundamental human right—to respect customary law, it cannot be at the expense of subsuming rights of equality that exist in international law and also that apply in Fiji under the Constitution. Section 26(8)(g) of the Constitution of the Republic of Fiji provides that custom will apply unless "inconsistent with a provision of this Constitution or a statute, or repugnant to the general principles of humanity."

As mentioned, in the pursuit of strengthening women's resilience, land plays a key role in the ability of women and men to bounce back from shocks, and under the Constitution, women have equal rights to own and use and inherit land. Despite its complex nature, land ownership and control of land use needs to be critically examined from the perspective of gender equality, and efforts to promote women's access to assets needs to be included in laws and policies related to climate change and disaster risk.

2.4.3 General Improvement of Decent Work for Women

The final socioeconomic area covered in this report is decent work. As defined by the International Labour Organization (ILO), decent work encompasses "opportunities for work that is productive and delivers a fair income, security in the workplace and social protection for families, better prospects for personal development and social integration, freedom for people to express their concerns, organize and participate in the decisions that affect their lives and equality of opportunity and treatment for all women and men."[126] The key issues selected for this report that affect decent work for women in Fiji are sexual harassment and discrimination in employment, and lower remuneration compared to men doing work of the same value. These issues impact women's ability to gain and remain in decent work, and to build the economic security necessary to manage shocks caused by climate change and disasters.

Fiji has three laws that address sexual harassment in the workplace. The Employment Relations Act 2007 (Rev. 2019) section 76; the Human Rights and Anti-Discrimination Commission Act 2009 Section 19(2); and the Crimes Act 2009 (Rev. 2018) sections 207–213 on sexual and indecent assault. Each has different procedures and remedies. There is also a 2007 National Policy on Sexual Harassment in the Workplace that describes and amplifies the meaning of sexual harassment in the workplace and outlines each of the procedures under the three laws. The laws themselves do not have a definition of workplace sexual harassment, but the 2007 National Policy has a CEDAW-aligned description of sexual harassment in the workplace and additionally provides some practical, good practice guidelines of the types of conduct that would be included. Despite the laws in place, the CEDAW Committee—in its Concluding Observations—noted that in practice there was severe underreporting of sexual harassment in the workplace and that a relatively high number of employers did not adhere to the obligation of having a sexual harassment policy.[127] The 2020 ratification by Fiji of the Convention on Violence and Harassment in the Workplace (C190) shows a positive step toward addressing this critical issue[128] and implementation—including reviews of national laws and policies—will be essential.[129]

The second issue of decent work covered in this report is that of the gender gap in employment and equal pay for work of equal value. The CEDAW Committee noted that although women's employment and labor force

---

[125] CEDAW Committee. 2016. *Consideration of Reports Submitted by States Parties under Article 18 of the Convention – Fifth Periodic Report of States Parties Due in 2014 – Fiji.* (A/70/38). New York.

[126] ILO. N.d. *Decent Work.*

[127] CEDAW. 2018. *Concluding Observations on the Fifth Periodic Report of Fiji.* CEDAW/C/FJI/CO/5 (14 March). para. 41(a). (CEDAW noted that the then Employment Relations Promulgation of 2007 did not apply to members of the armed forces, police or correction service. This remains true in the Employment Relations Act Section 3[2]).

[128] ILO. 2017. *C190 Violence and Harassment Convention, 2019 (No.190).* Geneva.

[129] FWRM. 2019. *FWRM Submission on the Ratification of the Violence and Harassment Convention 2019.* Suva.

participation was growing in Fiji, they remained low and that the pay gap between men and women is the widest in the Pacific region. The committee noted that women are frequently subjected to occupational segregation with accompanying wage differentials and are concentrated in lower-paid jobs, informal or unpaid work—even within the same industry—causing the wage differential to persist.[130]

Although Fiji has also ratified ILO Convention 100, it has not adopted nor enforced the principle of equal pay for work of equal value.[131] The Employment Relations Act was amended in 2015 to include section 78, which reads, "an employer must not refuse or omit to offer or afford a person the same rate of remuneration as are made available for persons of the same or substantially similar qualifications employed in the same or substantially similar circumstances on work of that description for any reason including..." and then refers to discriminatory grounds. The Committee of Experts on the Application of Conventions and Recommendations of the ILO in an observation published in Fiji in 2019, noted that section 78 still does not give full legislative expression to the principles of the ILO convention.[132] It still fails to comply with the convention requirements for the following reasons:

(i)   The convention refers to "work of equal value", which is to ensure equal remuneration for work or working conditions that may be different but of "equal value." Conceptually, it is broader than persons having the "same or substantially similar qualifications" or performing "the same or substantially similar circumstances on work."

(ii)   Work of "equal value" may be as different as heavy lifting of machinery parts in a factory (often done by men) and dexterity in inserting parts into machines in a factory (often done by women). The qualifications of each may be very different and they are not employed in the same or substantially similar circumstances.

The convention through its provisions addresses gender stereotyping of jobs. The committee urged the Government of Fiji to rectify this deficiency.[133]

Other compounding issues facing access to decent work by women in Fiji include the ability to access minimum wage. Fiji has had a National Minimum Wage Policy in place since 2014 that covers 10 key sectors—including the garment industry—in which many women work under the Wages Regulations Orders.[134] In 2015, the minimum wage was increased, benefiting approximately 100,000 vulnerable workers. As of 2021, access is still not widespread enough to those who are likely most affected by climate change impacts.[135] A minimum wage floor could be extended to specific categories of work in Fiji, work in which women tend to be disproportionately represented such as agricultural workers and in some service industries. The CEDAW Committee also noted that Fiji should regularly review wages in sectors in which women are concentrated.[136]

Decent work includes important ingredients for strengthening the economic resilience of women to climate change and disasters, increasing women's participation in the workforce, improving the types of jobs they perform, and their remuneration for those jobs. Agriculture, fisheries, and tourism remain some of the greatest sources of employment for men and women in Fiji and are severely impacted by climate change and disaster risks. Decent work for women in these sectors is therefore an important aspect of women's socioeconomic resilience in Fiji and laws and policies need to be in place to support this.

---

[130] CEDAW. 2018. *Concluding Observations on the Fifth Periodic Report of Fiji.* CEDAW/C/FJI/CO/5 (14 March).

[131] Footnote 130. Para. 40(a).

[132] ILO. 2019. *Observation (CEACR) - Adopted 2018, Published 108th ILC Session (2019) Equal Remuneration Convention, 1951 (No. 100) - Fiji (Ratification: 2002).* Geneva.

[133] Footnote 132.

[134] Government of Fiji, Ministry of Employment, Productivity and Industrial Relations. 2014. *Annual Report.* Suva.

[135] Government of Fiji, Media Centre. 2015. *Fijian Government Increases National Minimum Wage.* 9 February.

[136] CEDAW. 2018. *Concluding Observations on the Fifth Periodic Report of Fiji.* CEDAW/C/FJI/CO/5 (14 March). para. 39(a).

3 | Conclusions and Recommendations

The purpose of this report was to conduct a gender analysis of the national legal and policy frameworks of Fiji to determine the extent to which laws, policies, and strategies consider gender inequalities in climate and disaster risk and contribute to strengthening women's resilience. The analysis found that Fiji has taken significant strides to improve its institutional and policy framework aimed at accelerating the elimination of discrimination against all women and children and promoting gender equality. However, there is further work to be done to ensure that some of the institutions that have been set up—and the policies related to gender and the implementation of the various laws—are truly having the effect intended by the government.

Newly revised laws and policies on disaster risk management in Fiji fail to recognize the link between gender inequality and disaster risks, and as such gender has not yet been mainstreamed. Indeed, the vulnerability narrative of women continues to dominate in laws and policies in Fiji. This is in contrast to the progress made to mainstream gender in climate policy, which is commendable. The Climate Change Act 2021, as well as the NCCP, are examples of how gender-responsive legislation can look. The approach of gender inclusion as a principle or goal is a feature of newer specific laws and policies on climate change and disaster in Fiji, however it is important to note that it is not carried into the implementation sections of many of the policies. Guidance may therefore be needed to support gender-responsive implementation and programming under these laws and policies, including guidelines and toolkits for government officials.

Gender-responsive disaster and climate change action are necessary to improve the resilience of women to disasters and climate change in Fiji, but these specific laws and policies operate in the context of broader gender inequalities in Fiji. The preexisting disadvantages mean that disaster and climate risk is a greater threat to women's socioeconomic resilience than to men's because women start from a position of having less secure, lower-paid work, and a high level of domestic violence and workplace sexual harassment that impacts their capacity to develop and prosper. Climate change and DRM laws and policies are also part of an overall national legal framework that can promote gender equality, reduce sex discrimination, VAW, and sexual harassment, increase economic opportunities for women through equal remuneration for work of equal value, and improve women's access to land, housing, and assets. This wider system has been discussed as an essential element to underpin women's resilience in the longer term.

CEDAW GR37 articulates a push for policy coherence and effective integration of gender equality within legislation and policies in sectors relevant to climate change and disaster risk. The framework developed for this report has provided an approach to identifying laws and policies that impact the ability of women to build resilience to climate change and disasters. The gender scale adopted in the analysis is an important tool to understand across multiple sectors where gender has or has not been mainstreamed. Based on the results of this analysis, a series of recommendations are made.

Specific Recommendations

(i) **Mainstream gender equality and the gender dimensions of disaster resilience into the new DRM Bill.** It is recommended that the NDMO with the Department of Women take steps to ensure that the new/revised act is gender-responsive, in particular by including a section on overall DRM objectives and/or principles. This should be similar to Part 5.3 of the NDRRP and include (a) gender equality, (b) nondiscrimination, (c) mechanisms for institutional representation of women, and (d) provision for necessary positive assistance that also accommodates biological differences based on the CEDAW definitions. It should also include a section on gender issues that recognizes potential differences in disaster resilience or impacts between men and women, and that women may bring different and important experiences to effective DRM. To achieve this, it is recommended that implementers be required to collect, analyze, monitor, and publish sex-disaggregated data, and allocate budgets, monitor, and evaluate expenditure to address gender issues in DRM.

(ii) **Acknowledge the links between disasters and increased incidences of GBV in laws and policies and support increased implementation of appropriate responses and redress for survivors of GBV.** It is recommended that NDMO work in partnership with the Ministry of Women, Children and Poverty Alleviation (MWCPA) to promote the inclusion of GBV–disaster links in laws, policies, and regulations, similar to the NDRRP's section on "Challenges Including Gender-Based Violence in Case of Evacuation." Together, NDMO and MWCPA can improve the capacity of national DM offices and other humanitarian stakeholders to intervene effectively to prevent violence, as well as protect and rescue victims during and after disasters. In line with the CEDAW Committee's concluding observations, this requires ensuring that "disaster preparedness plans include provision for setting up women-only shelters, where women can report cases of GBV and obtain access to redress and rehabilitation."[137]

(iii) **Develop practical guidance on gender mainstreaming in implementation and budget allocation for gender-responsive climate action.** The Climate Change Act 2021 has established a new law on climate change that will be the basis for policy, planning, and action on climate change mitigation and adaptation for many years to come. Adequate climate finance must be in place to meet the gender outcomes prescribed in the act and subsequent policies. It would be recommended to take this opportunity of the enactment of the act to establish a stronger base for resourcing and budgeting gender-responsive climate change adaptation and mitigation.

(iv) **Revise the Environment Management (EIA Process) Regulations 2007 under section 61 of the Environment Management Act 2005 to ensure women have equal roles in decision-making.** In the short term, it is recommended to revise the EIA Process Regulations 2007 to create a mechanism within the EIA process to ensure that women in stakeholder communities have an equal role in decision-making, including the opportunity to consult separately with women. This should be adaptable to the needs and wishes of women in communities where decisions are made under customary law.

General Recommendations

(i) **The collection and analysis of disaggregated data need to be prioritized.** Noted as the first specific measure under CEDAW GR37, the collection and assessment of disaggregated data are critical to understanding the complex impacts of climate change and disaster risk. This report has demonstrated that as of 2021, there is little disaggregated data and evidence to identify the gender-based vulnerabilities and the data that does exist is fragmented and not consistently collected or used. Collection of data

---

[137] Footnote 136. p. 15.

disaggregated by sex, age, disability, ethnicity, and geographical location at the minimum is recommended. Given Fiji's goal to avoid exacerbating vulnerabilities or deepening gender inequality under the NCCP, and the overall goal to increase the collection of sex- and age-disaggregated data under the NDP 2017, implementing this commitment across all areas of climate change and DRM will be critical.

(ii)   **Develop gender mainstreaming guidelines on disaster risk management and climate change to support the implementation of both the NDRRP and the NCCP.** Gender mainstreaming guidelines will help ensure that mechanisms are required to implement these policies, such as action items, action plans, monitoring, allocation of resources and evaluation, sustaining gender inclusion, applying a gender analysis, and collecting sex- and age-disaggregated data in their implementation. This could (a) provide a basic checklist for assessing whether a matter may have gender implications and for asking how the guiding principles have been applied at each point in the action plans; (b) set out the importance of collecting and analyzing sex- and age-disaggregated data and gender analysis, and examples of outcomes from such analysis; (c) include links to existing guidance and training tools on gender analysis, gender-inclusive consultations, and gender mainstreaming in policy drafting and implementation; and (d) be supported by basic training on gender concepts, equality, and discrimination, gender analysis, gender-inclusive consultations, empowering women in decision-making roles, and how these can be applied in the context of DRM and climate change in Fiji.

(iii)   **Develop guidelines on increasing women's participation in environmental decision-making.** As of 2021, women have very little say over the policy formulation process due to the limited number of women in environmental decision-making positions and a lack of mandate for gender-inclusive processes in Fiji. Both the NCCP and the Climate Change Act 2021 recognize this gap and aim to change it. Leveraging these commitments and laws and creating a guideline on gender-responsive consultations and participation is recommended. This can provide a standard for community and public participation that can be implemented at multiple levels and work toward increasing the voice of often marginalized groups such as those in rural areas and all women.

Glossary

Discrimination against girls and women. Any distinction, exclusion, or restriction made based on sex that has the effect or purpose of impairing or nullifying the recognition, enjoyment, or exercise by women irrespective of their marital status, based on equality of men and women, of human rights and fundamental freedoms in the political, economic, social, cultural civil or any other field. The definition includes not just **direct discrimination** (or intentional discrimination) but also any act that perpetuates inequality between men and women, which may be **indirect discrimination.**

Source: United Nations Entity for Gender Equality and the Empowerment of Women (UN Women) 2017. *Gender Equality Glossary.*

Gender. Refers to the roles, behaviors, activities, and attributes that a given society at a given time considers appropriate for men and women. In addition to the social attributes and opportunities associated with being male and female and the relationships between women and men and girls and boys, gender also refers to the relations between women and between men. These attributes, opportunities, and relationships are socially constructed and are learned through socialization processes. They are context/time-specific and changeable. Gender determines what is expected, allowed, and valued in a woman or a man in a given context. In most societies, there are differences and inequalities between women and men in responsibilities assigned, activities undertaken, access to and control over resources, as well as decision-making opportunities. Gender is part of the broader sociocultural context. Other important criteria for sociocultural analysis include class, race, poverty level, ethnic group, sexual orientation, age, etc. (see "discrimination").

Source: UN Women. 2017. *Gender Equality Glossary.*

Gender analysis. A critical examination of how differences in gender roles, activities, needs, opportunities, and rights/entitlements affect men, women, girls, and boys in certain situations or contexts. Gender analysis examines the relationships between females and males and their access to and control of resources, and the constraints they face relative to each other. A gender analysis should be integrated into all sector assessments or situational analyses to ensure that gender-based injustices and inequalities are not exacerbated by interventions and that where possible, greater equality and justice in gender relations are promoted.

Source: UN Women. 2017. *Gender Equality Glossary.*

Gender equality. Refers to the equal rights, responsibilities, and opportunities of women and men and girls and boys. Equality does not mean that women and men will become the same but that women's and men's rights, responsibilities, and opportunities will not depend on whether they are born male or female. Gender equality implies that the interests, needs, and priorities of both women and men are taken into consideration, recognizing the diversity of different groups of women and men. Gender equality is not a women's issue but should concern and fully engage men as well as women. Equality between women and men is seen both as a human rights issue and as a precondition for and indicator of sustainable people-centered development.

Source: UN Women. 2017. *Gender Equality Glossary.*

Gender equality includes formal equality (de jure equality – treating men and women the same) and **substantive equality** (de facto equality – equality of outcome for both women and men).

Source: Convention on the Elimination of All Forms of Discrimination Against Women (CEDAW). 2004. *General Recommendations Adopted by the Committee on the Elimination of Discrimination Against Women*. General Recommendation No. 25.

Gender mainstreaming. Gender mainstreaming is the chosen approach of the United Nations system and international community toward realizing progress on women's and girls' rights, as a subset of human rights to which the United Nations dedicates itself. It is not a goal or objective on its own. It is a strategy for implementing greater equality for women and girls in relation to men and boys. Mainstreaming a gender perspective is the process of assessing the implications for women and men of any planned action, including legislation, policies, or programs, in all areas and at all levels. It is a way to make women's and men's concerns and experiences an integral dimension of the design, implementation, monitoring, and evaluation of policies and programs in all political, economic, and societal spheres so that women and men benefit equally, and inequality is not perpetuated. The ultimate goal is to achieve gender equality.

Source: UN Women. 2017. *Gender Equality Glossary.*

Gender negative. Applies gender norms, roles, and stereotypes that reinforce gender inequalities.

Source: UN Women. 2017. *Gender Equality Glossary.*

Gender-neutral. Gender is not considered relevant to outcomes.

Source: UN Women. 2017. *Gender Equality Glossary.*

Gender positive/transformative. Changes gender norms, and roles and transforms unequal gender relations to promote shared power, control of resources, decision-making, and support for women's empowerment.

Source: UN Women. 2017. *Gender Equality Glossary.*

Gender sensitive. Considers gender norms, roles, and relations taking into account sociocultural factors, but does not actively address gender inequalities.

Source: World Health Organization (WHO). 2012. https://www.who.int/westernpacific/publications-detail/mainstreaming-gender-in-health-adaptation-to-climate-change-programmes.

Gender-responsive. Pays attention to specific needs of women and men and intentionally uses gender considerations to affect the design, implementation, and results of legislation, policies, and programs.

Source: UNICEF. 2017. *Gender Equality Glossary of Terms and Concepts.*